© Copyright 2006 Jean Christian.
All rights reserved. No part of this publication may be reproduced, stored in a retrieval system, or transmitted, in any form or by any means, electronic, mechanical, photocopying, recording, or otherwise, without the written prior permission of the author.

Note for Librarians: A cataloguing record for this book is available from Library and Archives Canada at www.collectionscanada.ca/amicus/index-e.html
ISBN 1-4120-7117-8

Printed in Victoria, BC, Canada. Printed on paper with minimum 30% recycled fibre. Trafford's print shop runs on "green energy" from solar, wind and other environmentally-friendly power sources.

TRAFFORD
PUBLISHING

Offices in Canada, USA, Ireland and UK

Book sales for North America and international:
Trafford Publishing, 6E–2333 Government St.,
Victoria, BC V8T 4P4 CANADA
phone 250 383 6864 (toll-free 1 888 232 4444)
fax 250 383 6804; email to orders@trafford.com

Book sales in Europe:
Trafford Publishing (UK) Limited, 9 Park End Street, 2nd Floor
Oxford, UK OX1 1HH UNITED KINGDOM
phone +44 (0)1865 722 113 (local rate 0845 230 9601)
facsimile +44 (0)1865 722 868; info.uk@trafford.com

Order online at:
trafford.com/05-2012

10 9 8 7 6 5 4 3 2

Table of Contents

Acknowledgements 4

About The Cover 5

Names 6

Introduction 7

Who Are We 11

What Is All-Being 14

Who Are You 17

What Is Soul 21

Soham 25

Spiritual History 31

Stages Of Conscious Development 35

Infancy 35

Childhood 37

Adolescence 39

Adulthood 42

Elder Adulthood 45

Elderhood 49

Death 52

Where Humanity Is Now 55

What Is The True "I Am" 57

What Do We Believe 62

Facing Pain 75

Ways And Places 78

Nurturing & Building Truth 84

Belief 95

The Power Of Prayer, Meditation, Ceremony, & Ritual 111

Ceremony 118

Devotional Music 125

Service 129

Devotion 133

The Brilliant Doorways 137

Foundations Of The Future 148

Karma - The Journey Of A Potter 148

Patience & Understanding With The Process 163

The Doctrine Of Oneness 171

The Place Of Self In Oneness 175

Do Not Judge 180

Which Bell Do You Wish To Ring 182

Understanding The World 185

Dharmic Understanding 190

Patience With The Process 196

Practicing Truth 203

Teachings On Meditation 206

Inner Guidance Thoughts & Mantras ... 224

Choosing To Watch 236

Studying The Great Teachers 239

Crossing The Water 245

Practical Workings With Self 249

Human Nature & Divine Nature 259

The Scope Of Becoming Truth 263

The Buddha Field 269

Self Acceptance 273

Becoming Truth 276

Acknowledgements

It is with true love and gratitude I acknowledge Nicole L'Orsa and Taylor Fox. These two have volunteered countless hours transcribing channelled tapes, editing, arranging the layout, and designing the book cover.

May the light of truth fill and bless you.

I also acknowledge my dear mother, Hazel, who has funded the printing of this project.

I thank the Ramana Maharshi ashram for allowing the picture of Mt. Arunachala to herald and grace the cover.

I thank beyond words the masters and holy teachers given to humankind throughout time, and for their words honoured in this book.

Love Jean

About The Cover

Ramana Maharshi used to declare that Arunachala was the spiritual axis of the earth. So definite was he that he once made someone get an atlas and see if there was not some other mountain at the other end of the axis corresponding to this Hill on the other side of the world.

Nandi said ~

> For Arunachala most holy is,
> Of all the spots on earth most sacred it.
> The Heart is of the world, know also this!
> Of Siva 'tis the Heart-Core,
> Both secret and sacred too,
> For here He dwells for e'er
> As the Aruna Hill beyond compare.
>
> The Poems of Sri Ramana Maharshi

Names

To all readers who are uncomfortable with the word 'God', I ask you to replace it with what feels right for you. Other terms equally as insufficient, such as Grace, Supreme Presence, Light, Eternal Beingness, Yahweh, Allah, the Absolute, all refer to the Unnameable Source of all Creation.

"What gives you light?"
"It is the sun by day, a lamp by night."
"'Tis what light knows this light?"
"It is the eye."
"What light knows this again?
"The light of mind."
What knows the light of mind?"
"Oh, that is I."
The Guru then replies:
"As such thou art the Light of Lights."
"I AM."

The Poems of Sri Ramana Maharshi

Introduction

I offer this book as a way-pointer
on the pilgrim's trail, a blaze on the tree,
an *inukshuk*, or simply a welcome arrow
painted on a board.

The mountain is rich in trails
winding their eventual way
into greater light and perspective.
I respect and honour all paths,
all teachers, avatars and way-pointers.
I place myself as a student of God
through all beings.

I am a way-pointer
and at times I am quite lost
and it is my child who is the way-pointer.

I am the channel for this book
and yet I am the reader as well.

I know we are all beauty
becoming aware of itself.
We are all God awakening to God.
We are all truth
becoming conscious of truth.

Grace is immeasurable, bountiful
and throughout all creation.

Let us celebrate Becoming Truth.

Jean

If I speak in the tongues of men and angels, but have not love, I am a noisy gong or a clanging cymbal. And if I have prophetic powers, and understand all mysteries and all knowledge, and if I have all faith, so as to remove mountains, but have not love, I am nothing. If I give away all I have, and if I deliver my body to be burned, but have not love, I gain nothing. Love is patient and kind; love is not jealous or boastful; it is not arrogant or rude. Love does not insist on its own way; it is not irritable or resentful; it does not rejoice at wrong, but rejoices in the right. Love bears all things, believes all things, hopes all things, endures all things. Love never ends; as for prophecies, they will pass away; as for tongues, they will cease; as for knowledge, it will pass away. For our knowledge is imperfect and our prophecy is imperfect; but when the perfect comes, the imperfect will pass away. When I was a child, I spoke like a child, I thought like a child, I reasoned like a child; when I became a man, I gave up childish ways. For now we see in a mirror dimly, but then face to face. Now I know in part; then I shall understand fully, even as I have been fully understood. So faith, hope, love abide, these three; but the greatest of these is love.

Corinthians 13, Holy Bible

As the scriptures record Moses and Jesus, we can imagine how the Buddha must have shone that bright spring morning in the Himalayan foothills. Dazzled by the radiance of his personality, it is said, people gathered about him and asked, "Are you a God?" "
No."
"Are you an angel?"
"No."
"What are you then?"
The Buddha smiled and answered simply, "I am awake" - the literal meaning of the word Buddha, from the Sanskrit root budh, to wake up.

Dhammapuda

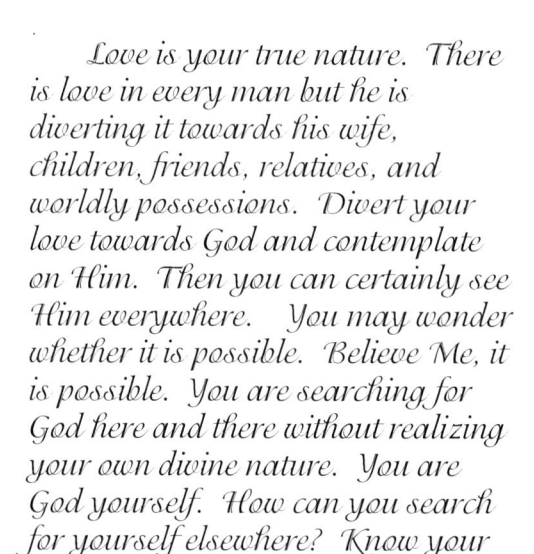

Love is your true nature. There is love in every man but he is diverting it towards his wife, children, friends, relatives, and worldly possessions. Divert your love towards God and contemplate on Him. Then you can certainly see Him everywhere. You may wonder whether it is possible. Believe Me, it is possible. You are searching for God here and there without realizing your own divine nature. You are God yourself. How can you search for yourself elsewhere? Know your true identity.

Sathya Sai Baba

Who Are We?
What Is The Truth Of The Human Being?

There is one being - the beinglessness, the all-pervading presence of consciousness. There is essentially only that - All-Beingness. Imagine a great orb of presence, a depth of awareness, a supreme consciousness pervading all matter and non-matter.

Imagine a great body that appears as the universe, saturated with consciousness and awareness in a million degrees and shades, from the most simplistic, inert and dull to the most exquisite and freed. Imagine this entire being, alive, pulsing with indescribable complexity, composed of all the forms, living and non-living, all the gases, elements, particles, limbs, eyes, ears - *all* the forms. This is who you are. You are *all that.* You are the entire being, all those forms, living and non-living, all those gases and particles. You are the universe and you are beyond the universe.

The description of who you are is vast and complex. It is most difficult to grasp and yet utterly simple. If you use your linear mind, if you step into the task of understanding from your present mind base, you will not be able to. It is too vast. Yet if you breathe into the truth within your being, the essential place of true knowing and awareness, you will understand instantly. You will feel, you will experience, that you are *all that*. You are all beings, all matter. You are unconfined by birth and death, by lives. The answer of who you really are goes on and on. It opens your being until you have no separation left, no protection, no isolated singular self, no name. And yet it opens you up to joy, to freedom, to everything. It is an important question to ask and keep asking. And yet realize you will only truly understand by entering into the experience, the core of your truth, into all that which, if it is truth at all, you are able to enter.

Truth is findable and affirmable by your own experience. You needn't accept this from a book or from the words of another. You cannot. You can only accept this by knowing, by experiencing the vastness of All-Being, of God. You are not separate from God, or a faulty factor evolving towards God. You **are already**, always have been and always will be.

"Who then is God?"
"The witness of the mind."
*"My mind is witnessed by myself,
the soul."*
"So you are God."

*The scriptures also state
there is but one God,
witness of All,
hidden in all creation,
Absolute,
pervading All,
the Inner Self of All.*

The Poems of Sri Ramana Maharshi

What Is All-Being?
What Is God?
What Is Truth?

Words will be placed towards this, yet remember the real answer is an experience. It is experienced by becoming it, by remembering it, by breathing into and realizing it wordlessly. It has been shown to you by the masters, yogis, Brahmans, and the beings who have entered into realization of their true nature. It has been shown to you time and time again. Look at it. Observe it, watch it, study it. It is not new. Once having experienced the true nature of God within your being, there is no turning back. The expansiveness, the peace, the deep sense of satisfaction, the freedom from self and bondage and suffering is most convincing and needs no struggle for acceptance. It is the great fruit of this whole creation that when any part realizes the whole, it realizes the truth.

What is this truth? What is God? 'God' is the presence of the most exquisite love. Imagine the most beautiful of beauty, the most gracious of grace, the most compassionate and kind. Imagine that which sits in exquisite perfection, in harmonious existence, that which is all and excludes none, that which has unquestionable purpose in its existence. That is God Presence.

Imagine the most brilliant yet soothing and nurturing light, the joy without passion, the peace beyond understanding, the "I am" without boundaries. Not the "I am" that sits apart from all other beings, but the "I am" that resounds within all beings. That is God Presence. That which sits apart is also God, for all form and shadow, harmony and chaos, brilliant and dark, is Truth and All-Beingness.

Why does a flower need to create petals in order to propagate itself, to attract? Why does nature need to be manifesting with such beauty? That is God. Beauty is God. God in its most crystallized perfection of clarity and beingness is beauty. God in formation, god in unconsciousness, in development, is that which shows itself as untruth, as unbeautiful.

God can be understood at different points of evolution and formation. Consciousness sits dully, inert, in stone. Realize the dynamism of what God is, of what you are. Realize even in shadow this vast being called "All-Being" or "God" is growing, moving, pulsing. Imagine the surface - the most refined, developed aspects of God speaking in the avatars and masters, speaking from angels, being portrayed most beauteously. Imagine the aspects of the god-body that are infantile, dull, and in unconsciousness, that cannot hear the voice of beauty, cannot see it or create it. It is all you; it is all God. It is all a living, growing, dynamic being and you are not separate.

The eye cannot see it;
The mind cannot grasp it.
The unchanging has neither
Eyes nor ears,
Neither hands nor feet.
Sages say it is infinite in the great,
And in the small,
Everlasting and changeless,
The source of all life.

As the web issues out of the spider
And is withdrawn,
As plants sprout from the earth,
As hair grows from the body,
Even so, the sages say,
This universe springs from the
Imperishable, the source of all life.

Mundaka 1.1.6-7
The Dhammapada

Who Are You?

The question is potent. Ask it. Who am I? Am I this name, this form, this life, this mother? Am I this profession? What names have you given to yourself? How do you define who you are? Do your definitions create separation from all those around you? If so, your definitions are untruth. They are just passages of your being, expressions of God through the uniqueness your being.

Allow this. God must manifest in a million billion ways. Each way is unique, and we call that uniqueness a "self". It is giving the structure a name and a lifetime and in this potent formula it expresses something unique and definite and this is good.

Self is a part of God. Self is a part of the expression and self is a prison. When one only believes in this structure of self - the fire, will, emotion and mind - saying, "I am this and that's all", self has created a prison, an illusion and an untruth. Self has created a dead end, continuing to invest energy into maintaining separateness.

Who are you, really? The self is but a unique expression of divine nature, of God, flowing through one specific channel. Understand that addressing the truth creates a greater stream of expression, a river of greater experience. The self is then at peace and knows its place. It can express the highest principles, the most beauteous aspects and refined expressions of God in its evolving wholeness. Imagine the exquisite detail, the intricate beauty of consciousness that <u>knows</u>, that is in conscious truth. When the human being realizes this, it becomes this intricate beauty. It becomes a freedom that is no longer bound and confined in separation and is freed from its prison.

To see the Lord as other than the Self is but a mere projection of the mind. That man loses ego first of all and finds his birth-place, finds the seeing Self, 'tis said that that man has discovered God, because God is none other than the Self.

"To see oneself," is also "to see the Lord," the scriptures counsel. But what do they mean, for how to see the self? The Self is one. If one's unable even to see oneself, how then can one see God? Nay, 'tis the truth, the ego must indeed become His food.

God shines within each little intellect and brightens it with His almighty flame. How else can He be known by intellect than by the act of introverting it and merging there in perfect unity with God the Infinite, the Light of Lights?

The Poems of Sri Ramana Maharshi

Forgetting his innate divinity, man searches for God in the external world. God is within you. In fact, you are God yourself. For example, you are sitting here. Is it possible for you to find yourself outside? Is it not foolishness to search for yourself in the outside world? Look within; only then can you find God. It is very easy to understand your oneness with God. However, you should have firm faith to begin with. You should develop faith that God is not separate from you. When you enquire deeply, you will realize that God is in you and also outside.

* * * * * * * * * *

You are making various efforts to experience divinity. Do not search for God outside. He is in you. Everything is in you. All that you see outside is illusory. Do not be carried away by the illusory world. You do not need to study scriptures to know this simple truth. Develop inner vision and visualize your true Self. Enjoy the taste of divinity within. Only then can you attain peace and ultimately realize the truth, "I am I".

Sanathan Sarati
January 2004

What Is Soul?
What Is The Atma?

We show her a window, clear, blue, and crystalline. In that window is all creation - all that underlies it, all voices that speak, all beings that move or don't move, creation in all its forms. The window is the atma, the soul that sees. Hold that thought - the soul that sees.

The consciousness that is *conscious*, the eyes that can see the whole, the soul, the atma, is the consciousness of creation. Through that consciousness is a knowing - *I am. I am all that. Yet I am the one that says 'I am.' Yet I am the window that says, 'I am all that'. I am both all that and the one that can stand apart and say, 'I am all that.'* Consciousness arises to such totality that it says, "*I am all that*", and can feel its beingness as the whole beingness.

The soul, the atmic consciousness, is that window, that aspect that can look at any part of creation, see it, know it, and say, "I am that", to it. It can know and understand and see the rock and say, "I am", to the rock, comprehending deeply what that means. The soul, then, is not in separation, or a being apart from all other beings, but is simply the consciousness that can say, "I am." When one sits in the atmic soul saying, "I am", there is no sense of "I am separate from that 'I am', from those eyes that see, from that window." One sees those eyes and that window out there as "I am that - only one window, only one pair of eyes."

A unique character may surround, name, and give expression to the soul, may create and execute the journey of the soul's movement into explicit consciousness. Yet the personality, or character, is not the soul. It is only the growing, the process of creation on its way to "I am all that", the evolving of the entire being from the most dense, unconscious state to the most conscious. The soul, the atmic consciousness, is the most conscious state. The personality, physical form, and emotional nature are the substance of the soul percolating into absolute consciousness. They are the journey, not the destination, not the essence of the journeyer. The personality is the journey. The body is the journey. The soul is the one who journeys. The human character is the clothing, the medium of expression and force of evolution. Emotional pain and physical form anchor into lifetimes, creating momentum and forcing the soul towards its true awareness. This entire treatise is about this, the atmic truth, the "I am all that."

The soul has an inherent knowledge of itself. In the beginningless beginning, in the eternal middle, and in the endless end the soul has an inherent knowledge of itself. Potential, as though all is contained at all times, the perfection of God, of creation in full consciousness, is all there and yet still evolving.

So in this there is movement, momentum, pain, lives, ages, and evolution as inherent knowledge strives to rise into absolute knowledge, precise and crystalline.

It is as though every stone, every form of creation, strives towards this absolute freedom. And in the striving, hunger, movement, and yearning, the ages turn; the suns explode and cool, the universe is formed. Every gas and every particle, every atom of every body is this process. Every atom and gas and particle has contained within it the inherent knowledge of truth.

Truth is before form. Truth is free of form. Yet consciousness of truth, absolute manifestation of consciousness, requires form, requires the journey. The stones, plants, animals, planets, gases, particles, atoms, eyes, voices, hearts, pain, lives – it is all the great turning wheel.

*Be bound to the Atma in you.
Take rest and refuge in that;
meditate on that, without
interruption. Then, all bonds will
loosen of themselves, for the bond
with which you attach yourself to the
Lord or the Atma has the power of
unbinding all other bonds.*

*Sanathan Sarati
May 2004*

Soham

To understand the soul, the atmic consciousness of all-beingness, one cannot apply mind or words or books. One cannot apply feeling or emotion. One cannot study. One must breathe and move into the experience itself, into the inherent knowledge sitting there passively, quietly. Within every cell, every particle, every being, and within the human being with its capacity for consciousness, the atma can be experienced like a bright light.

The window has cleared. It is like a crystalline lens without occlusion. The pathways of consciousness are set within the brain. Evolution has carried this form of creation to a readiness to know itself, to know the whole truth. Yet 'to know' is not to apply the intellect. It is not to apply the self, the ego nature. To understand is to enter and be it, to allow the awakening in its simplicity to occur within the breath.

Soham - the Sanskrit sound of "I am this." "So" is the in-breath, "ham" is the out-breath. Every moment you are saying it, every moment you are breathing it. It is as simple as the breath and listening.

All forms of creation hold soul, and yet the consciousness patterns have not all developed, cannot be utilized or are not there. There are gradations of potential of awareness throughout all forms. Understand, beautiful embodiments of love. Understand, human being, who you are.

<u>You are creation that is ready to know.</u> You have mapped within your being every intricate little pathway that is needed to know. You have the crystalline window, the lens that can see the whole being that you are. And yet it is so magnificent and vast and tremendous that it takes centuries and eras and ages for that very same human being. It's in one breath – Soham. And yet in thousands of epics there is no knowing of this. There is life after life of not knowing, of being caught and bound in "I am mind and emotion. I am body and I am separate."

Such is the purpose for this work. It is as simple as listening to the breath. To know soul, to experience the atmic truth, is as simple as sitting and listening to the breath, over and over, like the softest lullaby, the whispering simplicity of truth. As the mind quiets and as the emotion quiets, your being begins to know itself, to hear its eternal, endless presence.

Breathing into the body and out, visiting the form and leaving it, the atma is eternal. It is inherent knowledge from the beginningless beginning, the eternal middle and the endless end.

God permeates the entire universe. God is present in all beings in the form of their life-breath. He manifests in man's breath as Soham. Each inhalation signifies 'So' and each exhalation, 'Ham'. Every moment this process of inhalation and exhalation reminds us of our inherent divinity. 'So' means 'That' (God). 'Ham' stands for 'I' (individual). Though these are two words, namely God and individual, there is no difference between them. They are one and the same.

Sanathan Sarati
January 2004

Do not claim the soul as that which is named and separate, your character that sits apart from other characters, which shapes itself into a separate body and life. Do not carry that illusion, that the soul is a greater personality, claimed by you as you, separate from others. That grandeur is not truth and it is no grandeur at all to embellish the separateness, the greatness of this soul or that. There is greatness to the human being in its individual expression; there is greatness to the personalities that have taken shape as the journey. But the soul is a greatness beyond any of that. The soul is a tremendous, throbbing oneness of All-Beingness, claimed by none in separation. The soul is the great Aum, the "I am" that excludes nothing, that cannot be named or chronicled through thousands of epics of lives.

When a being merges with that window of "I am that," the personality and uniqueness of expression of a character dissolve and are no longer necessary, wanted, or mourned, dissipating like a mist in the morning sky. The sky is enough, for it is everything.

Now, if there is need to wear the robe of personality and character to demonstrate truth, to emanate and beam it into the evolving humanity, then it can be taken, but it is not bondage. It is simply put on, worn, used, and loved, but with no attachment, bondage or need. Indeed, it is like a wardrobe. One could put on different robes, different characters or faces, according to the need to communicate divine truth - the grace, the tremendous teaching that humanity needs to understand itself, to understand the actions to choose and not to choose, the thoughts to think and not to think. Don't feel that you will mourn the loss of identity, character or personality. You will have the entire wardrobe to choose from! When you are unbound there are all colours. When you are unbound there is only joy. There is a great array of creative possibilities for existence.

When you understand the atmic consciousness, breathing in the centre of your being, you will not cling or hold onto any vestige of personality or character. And though it may be a slow, gentle process, there is a widening and opening within your being that doesn't need to say this or do that, doesn't need to be seen, doesn't need the identity. It has found the only identity. When the morning mist dissolves into the morning sky, the sky is enough, for it is everything.

There is a reasoning that binds and there is a reasoning that liberates. He who sees the world as world, sees wrong. He who sees the world as Paramatma (God), sees right. The world is an effect that has a Cause; it cannot be differentiated or separated from Cause (God). It is just a mutation of Brahman (God). The millions of beings are the branches, twigs and leaves of a tree; the seed is Brahman in which the whole tree is present. He who knows this knows the Vedas (scriptures).

Krishna

Spiritual History
& The Evolution
Of The Human Being

Picture this universe; picture the suns, planets, and moons. This huge, enormous body of matter - picture it. See on this planet the ages, the volcanoes, the seas, the ice. Let the picture sweep through your consciousness. It is all the same being. The steaming, tropical climes, the grinding ice, the gaseous planets and unimaginable atmospheres – they are all the same being, all one body.

Let your body know this, not your mind. Let your breath know this. Because you have eyes to see and ears to hear, you are outside of what you see or hear. Do you know that the substances of creation that have no eyes or ears do not know themselves as outside but as part of? When this great body of beingness began to form eyes and ears, or shall we say awareness, the awareness of separateness began, looking upon from outside, as though separate from what is being looked at. As the consciousness needed to find ways to protect the form that the eyes were looking through, there deepened the sensation of separateness, and the primal fear to keep that form intact.

The story of separateness is very deep. It is as deep as the plants, the unicellular beings, the first creatures with the first eyes and the first brains, for there is truth in separateness. In the story of matter, there is this and that; this eats that, and so that has learned to protect itself and this has learned to consume that in order to protect itself and exist at all.

Matter required a fragmenting into a million changing, evolving forms. Picture the myriad forms. The vastness - your mind can only grasp what you've seen or heard in the age that you're in from the books that you read, and it is *much* greater than that. Do you know the forms that exist on other planetary bodies and gaseous planets? In this universe, you have the tiniest fragment of knowing of those forms, and that vastness of forms is telling you the vastness of who you are, the vastness of God, of truth and of what this Being is, the vastness of the evolution of consciousness. To maintain "I am a separate being from all other beings", is to stop short from ever knowing the truth, to be caught in matter's dictates, necessary actions, belief systems, and protections.

The soul has inherent knowledge of who it is, slowly budding, moving, stirring, becoming aware through the forms that it is held within. It is known more greatly upon the death of forms than through the birth, and as the forms go through their endless deaths, this inherent soul understands the eternal presence.

Do not let the human being be held as a separate evolution and a separate story from all evolution and all beings and forms. Rather, allow the human being to be one aspect of that form that is developing toward a greater and greater conscious ability, truly a flower within this sphere. The brain of the human being has been in long formation. Before it could ever be called human, this brain was forming through all the beings within this planetary sphere. This is the foundation, the backdrop of this brain you carry. There is the strong calling within the atma to rise into absolute consciousness in form. So then the human being is a form that is developing that ability. Through all the histories of all peoples and ages, watch for this consciousness. Was it there? How was that particular race being? Were they maintaining themselves in great separation?

It is necessary to think of the human being as a whole, as one great, tremendous being. Put aside for now the millions of individuals that compose this human being, and think of it as one great, evolving body of beingness. The patterning of one lifetime can be applied - the infant, child, adolescent, young adult, adult and elderly. These phases of a lifetime can be applied to the great being of humanity in its evolution of consciousness.

We will describe these phases of evolving humanity, and yet never get fixed thinking it is only one or the other. There is infancy occurring here while there may be adulthood occurring there. There are many races in the world and countless ages that these races have passed through. As you look about you with this grid of understanding, you can look towards a self, country, community, or race and see what stage of consciousness is being shown.

And yet even though all stages may be manifesting in different places throughout the world simultaneously, there is also a great mark or great theme of the ages - a massive time of infancy, or a massive time of childhood, so that the entire human being is actually moving all together through these phases. To understand anything is to look into a vastness and a wholeness that includes everything. To isolate a moment, or a particle, is to get lost, for God is a vast beingness. It is a vast evolution.

Stages Of Conscious Development

Infancy

We also speak of this being 'The Given'. It is given that the infant is absolutely merged to and part of the mother. The infancy stage of consciousness is not separate. It is undifferentiated and part of, inherently, unquestionably and necessarily.

The infancy of the human being was a tremendous time where God walked on earth through the forms of human beings. There was a great oneness amongst all beings whereby they did not think of themselves in separation, nor did they apply the yet undeveloped will towards individuality. God walked the earth with a magnitude, a beauty unobstructed by the human will and self.

The infancy was brilliant. Looked upon from the outside, it would look like great attainment, like wisdom had come, that God had found form. Indeed, God *had* found form; God was in form, unobstructed. It was a time of great manifestation, great skills, and great wisdom. It was as though a great source or pool of beingness was drawn from, an endless feast table was tasted, all the recipes for creation were available - a time of glory and a glorious beginning.

This time sits brilliant within those who remember, indeed within all beings for all beings *do* remember, in some way, their birth within this beautiful, bright sphere. The infancy sits as a calling, a demonstration of the ending, of what should be - the unity, the mergence with beauty, with All-Beingness, the unobstructed nature of all creation flowing into form.

And yet, if we were to zoom in on the human brain at that time, we would see it was greatly undeveloped. Alone, the human being would fall. Taken apart from the whole web, the human being would be a terrified, naked, useless and helpless being with no way to sustain or carry on. The infancy is a time of borrowing, from the mother and from God. The glory was borrowed and the human brain, the consciousness sitting within form, was not developed in its intricacy, in its capacity to hold consciousness, to say, "I am". It was as though there was a great thrumming "I am," but not a powerful speaking of "I am from God".

A strange story, really, of consciousness that needs to move exactly how it has moved, further and further into form, further and further into separation, and then to re-find itself with strength, maturity and awakening, back in union with All again.

So we speak of this phase of infancy as deep within the historical folds of life on this planet, a time and land that are lost, memories that are all but lost, standing so brilliant as to be unable to integrate, a time of glory, like a prototype of the ending.

Childhood

Picture a cell moving into division, becoming two cells - mitosis. The eyes begin to see outside and see that the one who is looking is separate from what is being looked at. There is the beginning of separation then, and this is truly the beginning of consciousness - looking about and realizing what is being seen in a very new way, feeling the stirrings of will, of decision, realizing most strongly the need for protection of the separateness, the form that is being looked through. It is no longer 'given', no longer assumed. There must be a basic, crude effort to exist, to protect.

This is just the beginning of these things for the child is still very merged, yet no longer with the great light, the great presence that is now directed towards earth. The child stage within humanity's consciousness is a very earth-woven time where the <u>earth becomes God</u>. The earth is being listened to as the messenger, as the great being one is part of. The earth is the provider. The earth is the one who punishes and gives, blesses and takes away. It is a primitive stage of conscious development, still seen today.

This is the child, and the human brain then has begun to develop a place of separateness which is ultimately the beginning of a crystalline, brilliant consciousness that will choose its way back to unity and no longer live in assumption, in the nebulous, warm womb of mergence, but will stand as a brilliant sunbeam and know unity.

There are many races that still carry elements of this child phase. They are beautiful and necessary and they are all a part of you. Merge with and be bonded to the earth as the gift that God gave, sustaining that reverence, listening to the earth as a living being. And yet don't be bound to it as the sole source of God or the sole aspect of unity.

These peoples that portrayed the child phase were also feeling very separate, one from each other, and would become very suspicious, would create boundaries. This was the beginning of using separation as an aspect of protection such as the animals do. If you were to study animals, you would understand the childhood phase well. They demonstrate both harmonious existence with each other as well as distinct and definite boundaries to the point of killing. Most only use those boundaries that would involve killing when necessary. It does not even occur to them, consciously, to use them otherwise. The separation, the need for protection, only arises in the obvious moment of need. It is not premeditated or designed and the rest of the time they're in a symbiotic unity with earth and all beings around them.

Adolescence

The next great phase of human consciousness development is the adolescent. As we go further into this, you will recognize more and more of what you feel and see. The adolescent staging of consciousness is the ultimate in feeling absolutely separate from all other beings. It is a constant need to protect, developing premeditation, employing the boundaries and tactics of protection well ahead of the moment of need, beginning to live in the structures, belief systems and identity of absolute separation and perpetually needing protection.

The adolescent stage of consciousness is war-like, ready to kill, fight, destroy or be destroyed. It believes that by destroying the physical form, the one who looks through the eyes has also been destroyed. There is the temporary belief of lifetime. There is no concept of eternal beingness, that the physical form is only a visitation being passed through. There is a strong belief that to kill is to end, and to kill an entire country will end that country's power, belief system, and spirit.

Adolescence is the age of domination. It is a time of tremendous pain, tremendous anguish. Do you recognize this stage of human consciousness? Do you find it within yourself? If you were to look within the human brain, you would see a bright energy formation around a very singular, condensed sense of "I am this." Not the "I am this" said while looking upon the mountains and lake and village, but the "I am this" said while looking only at one's own form.

This stage creates great strength within the form, great agility, and tremendous powers of mind. The mind is ever active, strongly declaring, "I am this" to all others. In every statement of "I am this" there is a boundary: "I am not that, and *you* are not this." There is a beauty in this adolescent, a virile, streaming, shining beauty. It is perhaps the most virile of the stages, and the one the human being has enjoyed for a long time.

It is easy to find the door into this stage of consciousness. The male lion, the dominant wolf, the king, the prince, the knight - we have many forms that demonstrate. And yet in this illustrious time of separation is the worst suffering, the worst destruction. Entire races of human beings are destroyed, humiliated and shamed, told that they should not exist, that they are nothing and worthless and not equal. Perhaps the greatest debts of karma are created in this stage of consciousness. And so the human being has been bound here, where karma must be carried forth. The wheel must turn around.

It is very difficult for the human being to leave this space, to return backwards or to move forward. Their identity is built deep and wide around this stage of consciousness. *I am this. I have a first name, a middle name, a last name; I have a family, I have ancestors; I have a lineage of profession, of actions; I have a hierarchy that I sit within.* Find all the identities, all the labels and names that you carry - they come from this phase.

As you look upon different cultures, you can see which consciousness phase is most manifesting. And when there is a large degree of that within the world, then that is telling you that the human being is there. Even though there are elders and sages, teachers and Buddhas, and always have been, the massive manifesting of consciousness occurs together. The human being is one great being. And those that move through the phases into the light, the masters, the enlightened ones, assist that growth. They nurture the human being forward as a whole, giving it religion, patterns, songs, pictures and understandings to urge them forward out of their bondage, forward into truth. Becoming truth - that's what it's all about.

Adulthood

*T*he next phase is the teenager moving into being a young adult. Don't allow yourself to become too fixed into definite pictures here. Realize all elements are there at all times, within you, within all beings. All voices can speak at times, and all can be seen here and there. The more conscious you become, the more you can choose and recognize and say, "Oh, that was the child", or "That was the adolescent." You can choose, "I wish to come as elder. I wish to manifest as adult," while realizing the beauty and creation that each phase is. Have patience, and honour the entire life cycle of the human being, of yourself, within this life and all lives, within the entire life cycle of God.

Now, as we sketch the young adult, we see eyes beginning to look outward, away from itself, noticing the beauty, feeling it stirring within, the artist, beginning to seek for the presence, the creator of the beauty, still quite outside of oneself, beginning to move into seeking God through prayer, ritual and ceremony, creating monuments and applying tremendous artworks to God, beginning to feel part of something much greater, wanting to drop this robe of separation, the dead end of death and war and domination, to drop that armour and become more expansive, realizing there is something much greater going on.

The adult phase of human consciousness means beginning to be prepared to nurture the young, to be in wonder at the infant and child, to look outside of one's self and see beauty, seeing one's self in that child, seeing one's self everywhere.

The adult phase of consciousness within the races of humanity create tremendous works of art and tremendous monuments, cathedrals, murals, and music that stir the soul deeply into its remembering: *I am part of. I was created. There is a great mother or father that I must sing to and erect lofty works of art to, that I must thank for my children and lead my children to.*

The adult is just as the word says, the beginning of a maturity within the human consciousness where that isolated chamber of separation no longer imprisons but thins. There is an expansiveness within the human brain that can receive higher information of what divine truth is, mostly through the forms of art. Through visual and musical and poetic art, the adult brain begins to receive the truth, as though from the outside and yet able to manifest it. There are great demonstrations of this through the magnificent artwork of the human being. If you were to look at that artwork, it is all aimed outward, honouring a deity or a great father or God that creates and permeates the universe, and that is outside of the one who is the artist, the one who sings. It is like a gift, an application to the great presence, to God - *Listen to me, hear me, lead me, bring me home.*

Awakening begins to occur within that human consciousness, without that particular being saying, "I am this art. I am this beauty." And yet that is what they're saying, for it did come from their own being;

it *is* the artwork of God they are painting, envisioning, living for. God painted, God created that cathedral. And yet the adult still feels outside of that divine being, laying monuments of beauty at the Unseen's feet.

Elder Adulthood

$\mathcal{A}$s one enters into an older phase of adult, toward the elderly, boundaries dissolve more and more. There is no longer such drive to create monuments into the sky, such passion to affirm God's existence. There is then that knowing that *I am he who you serve.*

Christ's words: *When you serve the least of your brethren, you serve me.* Service is the strongest tenet of the maturing adult. The golden rule - there cannot be a law more golden than the golden rule. *Do unto others as you would have them do unto you.* Oneness and unity, *I am that. There is only one being here and as I treat you, so do I treat myself. As I nurture and respect the earth, I respect my own being. As I see God in the waves, in the voices of people, I am listening to myself. I am god.*

This is a tremendous step.

So whatever you wish that men would do to you, do so to them; for this is the law and the prophets.

Matthew 7.12

As you look about you, you begin to see this adult moving into consciousness. The united nations, the sense of the world as a whole must be considered. There cannot be separation amongst peoples and countries. There cannot be separation amongst religions. There can be no intolerance or prejudice. The earth is seen to be one whole organism that all countries affect. All actions to do with world consciousness, seeing the world as a whole, helping the earth to be a healthier place, all political actions that strive toward communication and cooperation between all countries and peoples - all this is a sign of the adult, the adult that is beginning to emerge more and more.

This is for you to celebrate. As you look around, celebrate. Watch churches unite; watch countries begin to unite and work together. As humanity sees there is no future in war, separation, domination, greed, and pollution, the adult's consciousness is beginning to emerge. It begins to understand how one must serve another. One must work in service towards the whole at all times.

Compassion enters into this phase of the adult consciousness: being with, listening with, listening *as*, as though that person was myself; the beginning nudges, that person *is* myself, that country *is* my country, this earth is our country, this humanity is our brethren, and this God, by all its hundred and eight names, is only one. All religions speak the same language, and all human beings speak the same language in the heart, in the soul.

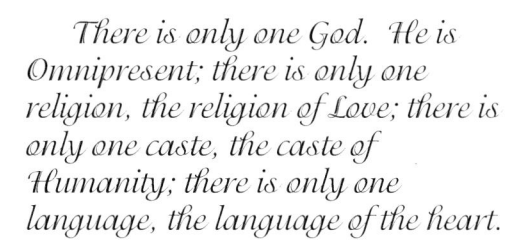

> *There is only one God. He is Omnipresent; there is only one religion, the religion of Love; there is only one caste, the caste of Humanity; there is only one language, the language of the heart.*
>
> *Sathya Sai Baba*

    This is the adult consciousness. The final lying down of armour and the true understanding of what "will" is to be used for. Will is to be used to create service. This is a time of great work. When the human being enters into its adult consciousness, when whole countries enter into this stage, there is great work, karmically. There is a cleanup job needed, a maturing, a responsibility, a teaching, a patience. Many of you who would be reading these words are here, in this adult time, needing to be patient with the karma that you have created, the karma humanity has created, working hard serving, erasing the errors, planting new gardens that will thrive and grow, planting new belief systems within your children, within your friends.

    Where is the human being, in general? Still, the human being can be found in all stages and yet the adult stage is fast emerging, being pushed upon the human evolution by the sickening earth and by the depth of the cry within the millions of individuals who carry such pain, who cannot tolerate war any longer, cannot tolerate holocausts. The pressure, self-created, that has poisoned the host and placed so much pain within the human collective soul, is pushing the human being into its evolution, into its adulthood. There is nothing amiss. It is all as it should be. It is when the sun is bright and hot that the plant goes to seed, knowing that it doesn't have much time left and that it must go into its next phase if it's to carry on. And so the human being has placed its own pressures of brilliant sun, of intensity, to ripen it further into its adulthood. It is good.

Elderhood

*R*espond; hear this within your own being. What does service mean? What does compassion mean? How can one's life be placed into service? How can one operate with compassion? Through service and compassion, pain is dissipated, karma is released, the past drops away and the future opens into truth.

The last great phase that we speak of here is likened to the elderly, the wisdom phase. Very seldom seen, as though no race of man as a collective whole has demonstrated this, it cannot be found. Let us describe it to you, so you can move towards it in your own life, so that you can recognize and nurture this final development. "Final" is an illusory term, and we will explain what we mean.

The wisdom phase is simplicity - not needing to manifest or create, not needing to be active, not pushed by pain and karma, not needing to demonstrate eagerly, with urgency, towards God. There is no God outside; there is only the presence of truth within all beings, within the "I", within the one who breathes.

The elderly phase is the consciousness of pure atma. It is the human being peacefully gazing upon the creation around, understanding exactly what is being seen, appreciating deeply the form of God in stone, water, waves and sky, not needing to *do* anything with it but observe and appreciate deeply and listen. It is a time of peace and deep consciousness of unity. It is the divine truth, truly walking, seeing both inwards and outwards simultaneously. It is a race of wisdom beings, of elders, and there will be a time when all of you will be there, gratefully observing beauty, within, without, part of, not needing to lift a finger for the perfection and intactness of God in form and God outside of form.

Truth is evident and known. The atmic consciousness has found a home in these wisdom beings and there is not the need to create "self." There is not the need to be confused by will or emotion. Will and emotion are understood and used in their place towards the whole, towards service and compassion, and towards the understanding that all beings are one being. The will is used to act, when it is necessary, towards service, towards those who need help, healing, guidance, or assistance. The emotional qualities that are always there have been transformed into a compassionate centre of knowing, where love flows like sunlight and emanates through the being, for God is love. Love is the core force of all creation and the emotional centre of the human being, as child, adolescent, and adult transforms into simply a site of compassion and the purest and highest love that knows no separation, no protection and sees all beings as itself.

There is no longer the need to move through the phases of the human form once the true understanding of All-Beingness has arrived. It is the beginning, not the ending. It is the beginning of true existence within the universe. It is the graduation from the narrow tunnel of developmental consciousness, and as the tunnel ends, the vista of possibility opens. It is no longer an end, as might be thought, of life and death and rebirth. But it is the end of bondage into illusion and untruth. It is the beginning of walking, breathing, existing in truth.

One could enter into a lifetime to serve, to illumine, to partake of the beauty of this world, or of any other world; to serve it, to help the entire being of God that is still bound in unconsciousness; to lift it much as the wisdom teachers of your past have done; to choose to exist within form for the sake of joy and service, to create more and more works of love in simplicity and peace. As this momentum gathers, the entire body of God moves into a glory, back into its mergence that the infancy stage was shown, a tremendous brilliant glory of I AM THIS, where each component of creation can say that.

This description now takes us to an edge of understanding that your brain, at present, is not even mapped for. To go beyond itself, beyond this human journey into an angelic, expanded journey of existence that requires an entirely new form - this is the edge that we end this speaking on.

Death

The seventh phase of consciousness development can be likened to dying, the releasing of the body. In this stage there is an expansion into the true being and there is no need for form; there is no need for the mind, brain, or self. The identity is centred beyond these forms in the eternal true nature, and then uses these forms as expressions of freedom, service and teaching, as though reaching back into the world of forms and selves to touch, lift, and teach it.

This seventh place of beingness is truly an ending of birth and death and the cycles of lifetimes. It is also the beginning of that new journey, the edge, which requires a new form and an entirely different mapping of consciousness to understand. The eyes of consciousness look from everywhere simultaneously, not fixed into one form looking out upon, but looking from all places, all the time, a sense of presence that is unconfined - All-presence. The stream of expression, whether it is through voice, song, touch, or movement, is able to coalesce into a singularity of beingness, a seemingly individual form, and yet does so only to focus the truth and love. A great brilliance can stream into a point that can then draw a line, a picture, can communicate into form or formlessness.

There is a freedom in this conscious stage that can move in and out of form, of individuality and singularity, not confined or bound, whereas at the beginning of this teaching, the infant stage, there is not this possibility to pointedly focus into form and use it as a way to draw a picture of beauty, write a poetry of truth, or create a lifetime of grace. There is rather a bondage to being disembodied, attached to source in an unconscious, given, assumed way, and an inability to move into the matter of creation and use it without becoming lost. There is no understanding of how matter is simply dust to be shaped towards the purpose of the highest grace. That is all that matter is for. Arrange the stones in a circle to tell the message of eternity. Place the words in sentences to speak the truth of eternity. Wear the face, eyes, and voice of a human being in order to walk the message of eternity.

Such is the purpose of the cycles of lives, the cycles and stages of consciousness - to bring the fool at the beginning back to the end, the story of the tarot. The fool at the beginning is ignorant, innocent, unknowing, deeply trusting without knowledge. The fool at the end has eyes like fire, eyes that see all, and trust from knowledge.

We wish to speak now towards your understanding of all this. You will see most of these stages of consciousness at all times throughout your history and present experience. You will see infant, child, and adolescent states; you will see it all at all times. You will see it all within your own being – You. And yet as a whole within your being, you have gathered yourself largely into one state, whether it is the adult or adolescent. So it is then with humanity, gathering itself at large into a stage of consciousness so that within any particular time period, and this particular time period, you will see all stages. You will also see the one great stage that it amassing and gathering momentum.

Where Humanity Is Now

*Y*ou are moving firmly into adulthood, but there are also great pockets of humanity that are strongly in adolescence. There are smaller pockets that are still in the infant and childhood stages – more so the childhood stages. There is a very diminishing presence of infant, and there is a great percentage of the adult. And though we would say this adult is coming into its prime, it is still in its younger stage. There is also the presence of the wisdom beings, the elders that stand as teachers and leaders throughout the world, standing in their own religious dogmatic paths, or standing outside of that. Yet they can be understood. It requires the adult state of consciousness to understand.

Within the span of this life on Earth, Perfection can be reached by fervent souls ardent in zeal, sincere in their toil.

*Zarasthushtra Yasna 51:12
(Founder of Zoroastrian religion)*

$\mathcal{Y}$ou are to have great optimism and hope, and more so great patience, for the evolution of the entire human being is a vast, deep, time-consuming process. To move from the adult into the elderly and into the formlessness beyond requires even greater steps, greater leaps of awareness than any before. To move into the eyes that see from everywhere, a being that can say, " I am you all", and is ready to relinquish self and separation – this is a tremendous process of becoming wiser and maturing. This is the process of becoming truth.

> *Being asked by the Pharisees when the kingdom of God was coming, he answered them, "The kingdom of God is not coming with signs to be observed; nor will they say, "Lo, here it is!" or "There!" for behold, the kingdom of God is in the midst of you.*
>
> *Luke 17.20*

What is the True "I Am"?

It is called illusion to live in a belief that is unsustainable, that does not reflect the true nature of creation, the ultimate reality. To exist in separation as self, emotion, individual, is to invest one's energy, consciously, physically, into that which is not true. This is illusion. There is power and process in illusion, but it must give way to truth. What is the true *I Am*? What is the true nature of self that is beyond the thousand million selves, that is the All-Self?

Mind tumbles and stumbles. The mind is geared towards separation, pointing its focus outward from I to them, from this to that. The mind is programmed to linear sight, to black and white, to rational conclusion and belief systems. The mind is huge in dictating consciousness. It was born in the childhood stage and came to its prime in adolescence. It is a slow castle to crumble in the adult. Seen through the lens of mind, the true being cannot be understood. It is as though one is looking through a window and seeing a blinding vastness of light, whereas on this side of the window, objects can be seen that are familiar and comfortable, called home. Through the window, looking with mind, it is an unrecognizable eternity of brilliance.

Mind dies when it moves through the window. It transforms in that light, loses its illusion of a coalescent self and character that exists as a separate cellular entity. The mind transforms into receptivity, All-knowing, all information of most exquisite depth - the knowledge of greatness. The mind becomes not a creator but a receiver. Through the window into the great expanse of light, there is not this need to create, to keep walls around one, to keep defined as separate and recognizable among others. There are no famous people, no hierarchy – that one who has nothing and this one who has everything. Mind strives to be something, to have everything. The mind is seldom at peace. Through that window, mind is at peace. It is a peace alms bowl filled to the brim with all there is to know, and the mind, which is the dictator to the emotion, speaks into the emotional centre of the human being a peace, a thrill, and a joy to be so much a part of, so much embraced.

  In the lower stages of consciousness, the emotion is struggling to feel this way or that, to feel rejection or acceptance, love or hatred, to be on guard, to relax – constant polarities. Like a cork in the sea, up and down - is it still? Is it wavy? The emotional place of being is continually reading – am I safe? Is it good? Are things going the way I need to keep my being intact, to be moving forward, to be okay? Is everyone okay around me that I love and care for? There is a constant emotional measuring of the environment and what is occurring around, and very seldom stillness or peace.

  Through the window, the mind has released its bubble and knows its place. And so does the emotional centre of beingness become a place where the river of love flows.

There is only that. There is only the deepest appreciation and gratitude, a recognition of the beauty inherent in all beings, all form, and all formlessness. There is a song of rejoicing that never ceases. The emotional centre becomes a place of compassion and giving.

Existence simplifies as it widens. Complexity comes from illusion, as the busy creation of separation, protection, and constant assessment of identity, validity, and place. Imagine thousands and thousands of human beings busily creating separation, protection, identity, safety, and place. It is loud. There are many hammers. There is much business, much bouncing back and forth, assessing how this or that person fits into my creation. Does this one oppose? Does this one support? It is an endless transaction with no resolution.

True resolution comes when a being lets go, is no longer uniquely, with great effort, placing its self outside of all other beings. It is simply in service to all other beings. It has found the expansiveness of freedom. It needs nothing and no one, yet needs everything and everyone. What we speak of is an incredible, astounding transformation of consciousness.

It will take humankind much longer, in the sense of time, to come to this great unity, to create within this world-dimension systems, families and communities based on unity, and to learn how to exist on the body of Earth as one with her and one with all. It will appear as tremendous beauty, yet also simplicity. Never again cathedrals of stone that reach up into the skies, cathedrals of great beauty that cost lives, that destroyed, enslaved and burdened. Rather, all will be created in a way that gives bounty, that holds peace in its roots and in its every step. Never again shall monuments be erected that supposedly speak of truth and yet cost the builders, defiled or lowered them. The human being needs to create nothing to know, to live in the grandeur within the breath, to exist on the planet because it is beautiful, and to exist to bring completion and peace to the place of evolving, and to watch those final chapters of what matter looks like when existed within from the place of truth.

     Great bounteous gardens, fragrances, the voices of birds – to exist within this realm, touching it all over, to its highest voice, to its most become – this brings peace to the place of evolving. This is your future and the more you can envision this, host it within your mind and imagination, and strive to understand it, the swifter it will arrive.

The Golden Path

The unconscious human
has only one path
the path of shadows

The becoming-conscious human
has two paths
the shadow path
and the golden path

The fully conscious human
has only one path
the golden path

Jean

What Do We Believe Of Who We Are?

This was spoken of earlier in the description of developmental stages within one lifetime and throughout the eras. This process of child to elder is really one of identity and learning how to identify with life, with soul, learning how to shape a bigger and bigger picture. Just as a child has a worldview as big as its yard, and is led to expand that further and further, so does identity expand. The beauty of the human lifetime, repeatedly, is that it holds all the stages within itself, a continual re-identifying with life, moving from the smallest to the biggest window possible by the time of death.

This window does not get very big in the human being very often. There are great binding limitations that do not allow a very big view. We will speak of these factors of limitation. Again, in consciousness there is freedom. By being conscious of these limitation factors, it enables you to see through them, to choose them or not. Being unconscious gives you no choice.

First we speak of the web of consciousness that you are in within your family, community, culture, peoples, country, and finally within the world as a whole, seeing it as concentric circles within that web. Most profoundly are you affected by the family web, the state of consciousness of those members in your family - what their belief systems are, and how they identify with their lives. Strongest of all is your mother and your father, for they give you the first map when you are most impressionable and needing to be written.

Outward from the parental influence are the other family members – grandparents, aunts, uncles - the family webs of your parents. This is very strong. The belief systems that are held in that family web are mostly assumed. They are called traditions – family traditions, religious traditions. And yet there are traditions that are far subtler than that – emotional belief systems, conclusions about what the world is like, its safety and its beauty.

The influence that a web of beings has on each other is very weighty. It gives very little room for the consciousness development to move. Belief systems are subtly, overtly, silently and loudly declared at all times, every hour of your existence. The human being is moved along by these belief systems like a sheep in the herd, unquestioning most of the time. If the herd goes there, so does the sheep. To move differently is a great risk. It can mean loss of family, safety, comfort, and support. If that family web of consciousness is found to hold great limitations within it, which most do, it is a risk that is not very often taken. When weighed against the risk of isolation, the risk of the limitation is small.

These factors of limitation are what hold the human being in a slow state of evolution. For eras, for centuries, very little movement is allowed through the individual being unwilling to take the risk, not understanding what it would be like. There is great compassion for this.

And yet when the belief web is highly limiting, if not destructive, there needs to be a force of change that cracks the urn, that breaks the web and scatters it. It may look like a most destructive event or series of events, but it frees the individuals. It requires all individuals within the broken web to begin to reconstruct their belief systems.

The force of dissolution is ever present within humanity's journey. Wars, holocausts, starvations, droughts, the influence of one culture upon another – all tragic stories in the minds and emotions of human beings, and yet brought upon by the oneness of the human being because without the forest fire, without the dissolution force, there would be virtually no movement or growth.

What we are saying is challenging. The human being very easily becomes stagnant, closed and still. It dislikes change or expansion and would rather close the curtains on that window and stay in the known. Look at a child – how many children do you know who are challenged by change, who would rather have the known day after day, have steadiness and continuity? Children need stability for their stage of being, to set their foundations into a steady ground.

This childhood stage of consciousness is still very present emotionally and mentally in the human being – too challenged by and disallowing change. One would largely stay in one phase for far too long were it not for this wind that blows in a new era of time, that is brought about by the momentum within that human being who must move forward into truth.

Remember the entire human being moves as a whole, as one organism. Therefore you can see one great change occurring in one part of the world that is very much like somewhere else in world that is cut-off by an entire ocean. Why is that? Because the human being is one being, and the change that you see here is the same change being seen there. The human being's consciousness and growth move as one.

The force of dissolution can easily be seen throughout history – fractured communities, torn cultures - as one aspect of the human being merges into another. And though there is wrongness and karma being created, there is also freedom being created as the human being combines itself.

We can look now historically, as one race of human being lives quite separately from all others, develops in purity and isolation, such as the North American native in relation to the Europeans. As these cultures begin to blend and move and mix themselves genetically, there is apparently great wrongness and destruction. Yet what is being broken is that stagnant urn that allows very little growth, that is in threat of stagnating to the point of shrinking.

In every case this can be seen. That group of beings needed expansion and growth. If you look at one day, year, or even one century, you will not see the picture. You must look from a scope that sees the whole, sees the genetic blending of cultures enhancing the ability for consciousness, enhancing the journey towards unity, moving the consciousness towards dissolving separation.

Dissolution then has been in place throughout time and has been very actively in place within the last several centuries. Letting go of homelands, of cultures, the fight amongst cultures and religions - there should be no fight! The voice of truth has been speaking within all cultures, all religions. Listen! Adopt that voice of truth as your own. Let go of your striving to hold onto a place. There is only one place – the world, and humanity.

Truth is only one. It cannot be two. Likewise, God who is the embodiment of truth, is only one. Ekam Sath Viprah Bahudha Vadanti (Truth is one, but the wise refer to it by various names)). You may call Him by any name, worship Him in any form, but always remember that there is only one God. You may call Him Allah, Jesus, Rama or Krishna but He is one. Once you understand this principle of unity and get established in it, you will certainly attain divinity.

Sanathan Sarati
May 2004

$\mathcal{T}$o let go of the separate hold on place, culture, race, or religion is to open to a richness that contains it all. You can hear the voice of truth speaking in all leaders, avatars, and prophets, receiving the best from all.

Look into the face of the native elder and say, "I am that."

Look at the mosque against the sky and say, "This speaks truth."

The world is yours once you let go, once you dissolve what you so passionately hold onto now to retain your safety, dignity, separation, and family. The world becomes yours! Every country has a treasure, an aspect of truth. You will never see the whole truth until you allow it all to speak.

Dissolution is to be understood and supported. It will only occur where it is needed. One can find peace with dissolution only when it is seen from the larger scope of the human being as one being seeking to find itself.

Consider the ornate, intricate beauty of that urn, full of the sweetest perfume, of innocence, devotion, and faith, a people immersed in a purity and a childlike staging of consciousness. Those people are you. What they hold there in that urn is yours.

Why was the urn shattered? It is not just a tragedy and wrongness. There is a purpose. The perfume, the Dalai Lama, is to travel the world. The perfume is to spread around the whole earth, and individual beings are to receive the whole world.

Do not be caught in the manner of dissolution for it most always will be terrible and wrong. Resistance and fear create the wrongness. Stagnancy, tradition, and holding on to no change eventually brings upon some great force of destruction.

And so all events can be seen on many levels. Yes, the Chinese were brutal and wanted land. But really the human being wants itself, no longer wants separation and stagnancy, wants to exist in truth. The most ignorant and greedy, land and power hungry, will knock upon the urn that holds the great perfume of truth. They will bring about the karma upon themselves that will teach them. The Chinese really needed that perfume for they had long forgotten and become stale within their box of confinement. They needed desperately that essence of truth that is that perfume.

Such is the beauty of the human struggle. What the person or country is really reaching for is what they really need. Eventually they will understand. What did the Europeans really need when they came to North America to conquer the "savages"? The Europeans was forgetting their ancient communion with earth. They were forgetting the simplicity and depth of respect needed towards the earth, towards their own bodies. They were becoming very unhealthy, very austere, building monuments that would go higher and higher, farther and farther away from where God really is. God is in the trees, the fish, the rivers, the wind and the ravens. The European was reaching out for what it really needed, stealing it.

What did the aboriginal really need? The aboriginal needed the higher structures of mind to focus his great soul, to empower it into manifestation. The aboriginal is sacred and deep, yet needed to be lifted further into the progression and skill of mind to manifest and comprehend truth.

All races need each other, need to share the perfume that they have developed in isolation. All races needed and still need dissolution of their walls, of belief systems that bar others from entering. War is the prime tool of dissolution at this time, struggling to protect and remain separate.

Soon the human being will realize the futility of this and will allow the dissolution to occur in a different way, willingly, consciously saying, "What have you to offer me? What are you bringing into my land? What is the richness of your teachers' ways, of your religions? Here are the riches of mine."

As the walls and barriers are allowed to dissolve, truth will be heard, stronger and stronger. It has always spoken the same language throughout the whole world, throughout all time. But the human being, in his reconstruction of truth towards its own end, will alter the words of the great teachers towards his own end. This will dissolve.

Fire will keep burning, and that which burns will burn, and that which does not burn will become strengthened and purified. The fire will keep burning in your life until all that must burn will burn, and all that will stand free of flame will stand strengthened by that very fire. Illusion burns. Untruth burns. Separation and stagnancy burn. All this will burn in all individuals, all races, all lands, and the fires will get very big indeed. The fires look like war.

Your task, individual reader, is to look at what must burn in your being. What beliefs systems are printed in your being that limit you? What have you assumed? What carries you nowhere? All individuals need to do this – examine the family, the culture, and the community. Examine the web that holds you in its fingers, suspended like a fly, binding you to this place. What belief systems will not burn that you value? Which ones will?

Again, the human being is held in stagnancy by this web of consciousness, being created by every being simultaneously, and though it moves slowly forward, it can move much more swiftly as each individual point within this web retracts falsity and chooses eternal, unchanging truth. As each individual steps into this journey of true becoming, so the entire web feels the ripple, hears the information. As each member in a family chooses to exist according to the wisdom they are hearing, the entire family is changed. If it can be done lovingly, confidently, and peacefully, the entire family is changed and graced by that one individual and is never the same again. Children coming into the family will never be the same, for there is this new light vibrating in the web that affects their being.

Remember, the entire human being yearns for truth, for beauty, for freedom. If it hears it, it moves that way. This is a law, written into the atoms and before-atoms of All-Beingness. God yearns to exist in absolute conscious manifestation. The human being yearns to exist in its true nature. It yearns for beauty. How do we see that? The human being yearns for wealth, fame, comfort, and safety. What do those treasures remind the human being of? Beauty, freedom – its true nature. The human being is reaching for these tenets of lifestyle that he is recognizing as the most beautiful, the most free. To be wealthy is to be the freest, to acquire the most beauty, become the safest. That is an illusion that will burn, just as the money and the house will burn, for true wealth and true beauty are not there.

The human being's true nature is an eternal beauty and wealth of existing in the light, in the gloriousness of freedom within. It is eyes that see the rose as a miracle and see all aspects of creation as incredible, vibrant beauty. It has no fear, no despair, no struggling for place, no protecting of moneys; it is not playing that great game of measuring. That is freedom, and that is joy.

Examine the web, the belief systems you exist within. What sort of striving is there for safety, freedom, beauty and place that are excessive? You need food while you are in the body. You need warmth and health. You need to surround yourself artistically and beautifully, yet with freedom, so that you are not bound or obsessed or fearful, or placing your efforts at too great an expense so that there is no inner peace, no time for joy, for realizing, no time to read anymore.

Examine the webs that you've agreed to, that you've been imprinted with. Does your religion allow the whole world? Does it allow all religions and all beings? Does it hold Grace to that extent? If it doesn't, then it will burn. Does it exclude any being anywhere and what they hold dear? Does it exclude their incense and rituals, their ways of finding truth? Does your work create pain for any being, for the earth? Does your way of insuring your safety and existence cost any other? Is your way of living pushing away realization of what others may be suffering in order for you to have what you need? Then you are caught in a web of separation and belief in illusion, and it will burn.

  As you negatively affect another being, you affect yourself, for there is no separation between you and that other being. And as you choose that which nurtures that other being as well as yourself, you live in truth and you free much more than yourself and that other being. You free the children that have yet to come beneath you. You free the family that will continue to develop after you have left. Do you understand the little web of your family and country, or the big web of humanity? One thread is you; one set of threads is your family. Whatever you pluck, whatever message you send along that fibre is heard throughout the entire world. There is no hiding, no exclusion. I cannot live in this way without affecting you.

  This great oneness is being understood more and more in this world where the oceans are carrying toxins from one land to another, airwaves carry information everywhere, commerce is one, political nations are too big for their land, and war here affects over there. The world is becoming conscious that it cannot exist in separation, that it is one web. This is a time of power, of fire. It is a time of accelerated evolution, and it is necessary and good. This is a time of dissolution of that which is false, and this is good.

Do your part and realize within your being what you sustain, hold onto, and believe in. Realize there really is no risk. The line is being come to where you will be pushed over anyway because the fire is beginning to burn greater and greater. As the human being feels pushed and begins to realize there is nothing to hold onto but truth, the web is burning anyway. The more willingly and consciously you can let go the more you exist in a strength, possibility, and maturity where you can become a benefit and a beneficiary, a transforming being, finding your own way to the feast table and the riches, to the realization of unity, rather than being forced and pushed.

Don't wait for the fire to burn so you have to leave. That is the way of immaturity. Rather, choose! Move with consciousness, with realization, peacefully. As the human being in general does this, there will be no more war, no fire. There will be a conscious and peaceful realizing of where life needs to go, what the identity really needs to hold, what the truth really is. "Of course, have this! Of course I will let you have that! Of course!"

Facing Pain

Pain is incurred through dissolution, through moving into a consciousness of the web, of the family and what is held in it, what you have agreed to without even knowing it. There is the pain that your mother held, the belief systems your father held and why, the great tragic drama of the human being trying to hold onto its past. There is a well of pain that is very deep and endless and it is for you to face. Realize it, for it is there.

Humanity has been screaming and crying, having to let go of its homelands, to emigrate, to become nameless, faceless cultures, to die of smallpox, to be put in residential schools, to be destroyed by alcohol, to be defiled as nothings, to be dominated, to be the child of the dominator, to BE the dominator! There is pain in every part of this story.

What is your story?
Where is your pain?
Where is your parents' pain?
How did the fire feel as their world was dissolved & what did they do with it?
How did they define & justify their pain?
Did they suppress & say nothing & hold a great white-hot silence? Did they rage & hit? Abuse & rape? Become disordered, bipolar, or sick & cancerous, unconscious & die?
What did your family do with its pain?

What is the message you received?
What did you hear?
More importantly, what did you believe?
Did you believe in suppressing & holding in pain like a white-hot silence that destroys the life force?
Did you learn to act-out & rage & dominate, to abuse & criticize, to push the pain away & make it others' faults?
Did you learn to be gracious with pain?
Did you learn to be ungracious?
Did you believe her, your mother, when she thought the world was terrifying & wrong & everything was to be feared?
Did you believe your father, that you must work constantly all the time to keep a safe home?

Did you believe that there was no God?
Did you believe that there was a God that punishes, that doesn't care?
Did you believe that your family holds a version of God that is right, & that the God of others is the devil?

What do you believe?
Hold that belief into the light.
Do you need to keep it? Does it work?
Does it burn? Does it survive the fire?
Most importantly, can you exist the rest of you life & into the lives to come with that belief?
Does it hold joy?
Does it hold the possibilities of beauty, an opening into a vastness of freedom?
Or does it confine you & hold you into stagnancy?

*T*his is facing pain. Ask these questions to feel the answers, to be unafraid to realize what you carry within you, imprinted from your family, from the generations before you. Use a journal to answer these questions one at a time. Illuminate the web within you. This creates freedom. Once illumination, which is a silent and beautiful fire, has burned that which is dead, false, and limiting, you are free to begin to know who you really are, what life really is, what All-Beingness, what atma, or soul, is, and all the words of truth become less necessary as truth is realized.

    As this journey is allowed, there is the movement into the wisdom beings, the freedom of the elders. Face the pain.

    If it is too big, there are ways being placed all over this world. There are those who will listen, who will guide. There are those setting up ashrams, spiritual centres for meditation, yoga, and inner realizing. There are many being called into service in many ways to help you face pain and dissolve the web. Reach out. The human being is seeking to heal itself, and is most beautiful in manifesting possibilities for this. Reach out. Find the new, vibrant, living web. There are those who will help you. There are programs and places. There are books such as this. There are more and more venues and ways to face pain safely, to let pain be a raft that carries you to a new shore. Listen into the true heart of the religions that offer ways that are life rafts through pain, the actual and original teachings of the founders, avatars, prophets, and divine ones.

Ways and Places

There is no shortage of ways and venues. Long have they been in place. When a being comes into any measure of realization, they begin to create a venue of service, a space of truth for others. In Buddhism, that is called the Buddha field. In India it is an ashram; it is called *to give Darshan*. It is to invite beings into that field where they can feel and experience the uplifted state of consciousness.

India is the spiritual jewel of humanity. Its riches are immeasurable. India gives Darshan to the world. Masters, prophets, and avatars come to the navel of the world and move outward. Buddha, Issa, Jesus Christ, Krishna, Brahma, Sathya Sai Baba, Shirdi Sai Baba – the list goes on and on. There is the path of yoga, in all its tenets and ways. India is a spiritual gift to you. It is spreading its teachers, voices, and venues around the world. There is no shortage of ways for you to hold onto that rope, that lifeline, to find the raft to take you from here to there. And this will increase.

Ashram and sangha mean "spiritual community". These islands are like hospitals for the soul. They are refuges and places to receive the new, living web that holds truth, to allow the burning of the old web. To go into an ashram is to invite the fire - Shiva, the aspect of God that burns illusion. As the world becomes one, so do its treasures become available to everyone.

Facing pain is not the same now as it was before. It was impossible to face pain before in the isolated communities where you would most certainly be ostracized, perhaps condemned by your church, faith, or family traditions. You are now in a most opportune time of humanity where the holds of tradition are becoming loose and the expectations to stay within the ancient webs of tradition are changing.

A great living master, Sathya Sai Baba, teaches: *do not leave your religion.* Accept the religious web you were born into, yet hear it for the first time. Hear the truth speaking. Not the human being speaking – hear the truth. What is the truth of Christianity, Hinduism, or Krishna? What did Jesus, Krishna, or Allah really say? Become truly a devotee to the religion you are in, to the master you have chosen.

Likewise, do not leave your family. Honour your mother, father, and community; yet bring to them all unconditional, true love. Transform the web that you are in with love. Choose truth within the context of your life. Choose love. Love the family that surrounds you. Bring to them truth, compassion. Be bold and courageous and speak of the truth that your family has adhered to, the religion it has devoted itself to. Do not enact tradition or untruth. Enact the truth.

Transform the web with love. Facing pain does not mean crying for years and centuries, or going into anger and resentment at oppressors or fathers or mothers, being angry with those who believe in limited ways, with abusers. It is easy to love your friend, but it is hard to love your enemy, as Jesus would say. Love is the only way of transformation that carries you into freedom. It is the only way to face pain: to have compassion for the belief systems of your family, of yourself; to understand why, how 'A' led to 'B', how this became that.

And yet realize your freedom of choice. 'A' does not need to lead to 'B'. Choose truth. Choose compassion. Choose the belief systems that lead into the high mountains, and if possible, live those beliefs within the family you chose. There is an important reason why. By leaving the family that you chose, you bring nothing to them. You leave a hole. You do not transform them, do not become the messenger, the one who gives and brings a higher freedom, a message of compassion and transformation to that family. By staying within that family, you lift them.

For some it may be necessary to gain a distance to hear truth, to transform the pain. And yet always try to at least hold compassionate and loving thoughts for the family. For some it is necessary to leave the family if they are destructive and too lost in bondage. And yet always send and give to them from whatever distance you have had to go, whether it is actual words or just prayer and compassionate, kind thought. Try to let the family know whom you have become and where you have gone to give them the pattern of one of their members that pulled the web higher into the light. Don't do this with arrogance or positioning, but with humility, service, and kindness as your intention. With courage: I am here because of truth.

If you love those who love you, what credit is that to you? For even sinners love those who love them. And if you do good to those who do good to you, what credit is that to you? For even sinners do the same. And if you lend to those from whom you hope to receive, what credit is that to you? Even sinners lend to sinners, to receive as much again. But love your enemies and do good, and lend, expecting nothing in return; and your reward will be great, and you will be sons of the Most High; for he is kind to the ungrateful and the selfish. Be merciful, even as your father is merciful.

Luke 6.32

*H*umility is most important. All beings are seeking the truth in their own ways that you may not recognize. Never impose your truth upon another; never declare you have found a better truth than another, for that is not true. That is more separation. To create pain in the name of finding truth is not truth. To create separation in the name of becoming truth is not truth. Separation is the hallmark of unconsciousness, of self-seeking. Unity is the hallmark of maturity.

Have compassion for family, for self, for its pain and journey, for the Chinese, for the Europeans, for the dissolving, the breaking of the urn, the cry of the breaking, for the whole story of the human being blending itself into one. Have compassion for the priests who abused. They were lonely and cut off. They were not who they thought they were. They were the children seeking comfort, just as the children they abused. Have compassion for the child seeking comfort, for the dissolving of the priest who was not a priest at all, for the fire that burns that which burns, for the European seeking its soul, its unity with earth, its simplicity, the aboriginal seeking to break free, to move into its brilliance, into the use of its mind in greater and greater ways, to break free of its confinement within its villages and traditions - compassion for the human being striving to become truth. The result is compassion for pain in you, in your brother, sister, mother, and father, in the drunk on the street, in the one in the jail, in the judge – compassion for everyone. They are where they are because of their place in their journey and what they have done with the pain of dissolution. Where they are now is not where they will be tomorrow.

You cannot judge. Do not judge! Listen to the teachings, the Ten Commandments – do not judge! These are ancient words of divine truth. Do not judge because you do not know, you do not understand the vastness of the story in front of you. Judging leads to more pain. Do not judge yourself, your mother, your father, or anyone. Do not judge! If you can realize how not to judge or criticize, you will have taken a quantum leap in freeing yourself from the web, and identifying yourself as "I am you, I am that". You are seeing your own story everywhere, and you are not separate from the story in front of you.

Compassion is the path to freedom. It is the way out of pain. Seek teachers. Seek sanctuaries, and the offerings that are there. There is no need to stay bound in pain, in patterns of painful dissolution. Once you realize this, freedom has begun. Peace; namaste; all my relations; Loka Samastas Sukhino Bhavantiu (let all the world have happiness and peace).

Nurturing & Building Truth

*T*he mind is a carving tool, a sculptor's knife. It shapes the structures and sense of reality for the being to walk into and exist within. The mind defines the moment and the day. It is a shaper, creator, deducer, and place of conclusion, of setting beliefs and deciding on realities. The mind seeks to be firm and linear. It seeks solidity, a belief that stays put, that moves from here to there and can be watched from where it came to where it leads.

The mind is simplistic in its force and tendency. In its primitive formation, it is geared to see and make sense out of what is before it, what is safe and unsafe, edible and not edible, what creates survival or death. Mind is a window that deduces and decides from what is, and finds the way like a guide or scout, saying, *"Go here, go there."* This is what is happening and also not what is happening.

The mind in a human being has become very cluttered indeed. It has developed foresight and hindsight, can create future scenarios of what might be safe or unsafe, what might work or not. It creates memory, a bank of knowledge from which to define and decide its reality.

The mind is a tool for safety and rightness. So in the human being, the mind knows - *if I go there, it will be like this, for I remember being there before.* The memory has set conditions that the mind works from.

The human being has become cluttered. It has developed mind in these ways, in great detail, deducing to the minutest degree in great foresight. What we speak of is a basis. The forces of the mind, the basis of mind's development, are always present even in the most sublime use of mind at present. There is always the measurement of safety, of value: *how does this serve me, how does this bring safety and benefit? Or how does this endanger and destroy?*

The mind is also a window of perception to understand beyond safety and danger, to purely comprehend God, the universe, and creation. The human being has developed this vastness of possibility within mind to use it for pure comprehension, but this is rare. There is almost always the underlying motive towards wealth, gain, protection, safety, and power. Pure comprehension has nothing to do with these forces.

The mind dictates the stirring, activation, or state of being within the emotion and the will. It is the scout that sees what is. The will is the responder to action or non-action. The emotion is the response to arrival. *Is it safe or not? Is it well or not?* The emotion is the place of sensing and feeling, of receiving information, the blind scout that moves with the senses, fully alert, feeling. And yet it is mind that makes conclusions of what is received. Mind declares it is this or that based on what the emotional scout senses. The will is that which executes action, carries out the decision. The will is that which moves the being from here to there.

This trio of faculties for manoeuvring within this sphere, for gathering information, perceiving it, deciding what to do with it, and creating actions - this is the soul's way to shape a life, a passage, a journey for evolving and understanding. These faculties clothe the soul.

If mind, then, is that which sees what is and concludes of the reality before it based on what emotion senses, then it is this place within your being where the most powerful shift can occur. What do we mean? If we just allow mind to make conclusions based on the information that comes, on the web we spoke of earlier, on the trained, emotional response, on all that comes from other human beings around us, then we remain bound in a belief system and a reality that may not serve.

We speak of how to use the mind to build and nurture the truth, and how to use these faculties of mind, feeling, and will. There must be a greater captain or scout than the mind and emotion. There must be a scout who has a stronger link to truth, a more expanded sensing and attunement. This greater scout is the soul, the atma, the eternal being that you are and always have been, is linked in all ways to truth and God, to the higher information and memory banks of creation.

By allowing the soul to be the scout and guide, the mind has a different role, as do the emotions and will. The mind is not making concrete conclusions based on a feeling that arrived that hour, or on the feelings in others around them. If you realize how cemented a belief becomes once it enters the mind and gets decided upon, you would see the danger. What you allow in your beliefs, how you take a belief easily from your feelings or another's, or from another's statements, and allow it to be cemented and written into your reality, your definition of who you are and what life is - this is the power of mind, to define and set a course, to believe wholly and firmly in what it holds within it. Yet it could believe this or it could believe that.

It is most important that the mind believe what is true rather than not true, for once the mind holds a belief, it cements it deep into the being, into the memory banks. It sets in place conditions that dictate to the emotional self and the will so that they act like servants of the mind.

In the chapter on dissolution, we asked that you look at what you believe, look at the belief web that you hold and are suspended within. Now we just speak of the power of this mind that has been developed and what it is to be used for. We cannot overemphasize how powerful this mind has become in its ability for foresight and hindsight, to go into great intricacy of projection, in its use of memory, developing realities that may or may not exist, ideas, possibilities that may or may not be true, and the power to dictate to the emotional self, the will self, and the physical self. *Is it peace? Is it health? Is it upheaval and sickness?* The mind sets the conditions by what it holds in its thoughts, beliefs, and core dynamics. The mind translates its reality into the emotion, which translates its state of being into the body. The will acts on what is believed and felt and takes the being further into that reality, giving more foundation to that belief system.

The human being, in short, has a great capacity to create around it and within it a complete and total reality. And yet does this match the true reality? Or is it an illusion? Does it create wellness, expansion, growth, and peace? Or does it create contraction, illness, and confinement? The very same tools and faculties create either. As the mind declares what is and holds a belief, the life span takes shape around it and sets that belief into matter, cells, the body, and all that is created around it.

The atmic soul, which all of you are and have, which is within your breath, beyond your mind, birth, and death, could be accessed and allowed to direct mind. Then truth would be created. The mind would see as directed from the higher plane of being. The mind would perceive and go into its creative faculty around what is true. What is true creates expansion, joy, wellness and unity. What is not true creates contraction, illness, separation, and confinement.

The mind will most likely, if left on its own, create what is not true because it cannot see the whole picture. It is not meant to, on its own, and was designed simply as a footman, a servant, a tool. It was not meant to be the captain, the guiding force. The mind, like the hand, emotion, and will, is a servant of the master, and was never meant to have the capacity of master. The mind is a sharp knife, a tool for carving, sculpting and creating a life, an understanding, a space and a place for the being to evolve within. Emotion is meant as a sensory opening to feel, embrace and love. The will was meant as the manifester, the mover, the ditch-digger. The atma, the eternal essence of beingness, is that which knows and understands most purely. As that is opened to, listened to, and allowed to flow through the faculties of the human personage, reality is shaped that is sustainable, that reflects beauty and truth, the beauty *of* truth.

Use the mind. Know what mind is for and know its power. Question its conclusions and beliefs and hold them up into a high measurement before letting them cement themselves into your being. Let the mind be like the page, the servant of the king, and let the mind say what is the most right, what is the most true, what leads to peace, what leads to harmony. Let the mind be a place to receive higher wisdom and knowledge, and once receiving it, let it form its beliefs and sense of what is reality around that. Let it cement itself around higher truth and set in motion within the body, emotion, and will these higher principles.

This is what the human being is for, to manifest the highest aspects of creation, the divine consciousness of great light, through mind, emotion, will and form. Realize what the emotional aspect of your being is doing. Take that emotional sensing but don't stop with it and allow conclusions to be made around it.

Perhaps somebody just came into the room with a dark countenance, a scowl. What did your emotional self tell you? Did it say you were in danger, or that you didn't like this person? That you needed to flee?

The greater truth is that that person is hurting, grieving and needs love. What if that person needed an embrace, needed some grace? Was your emotional self telling you the truth or was it responding in its primitive way? What did your mind do when it perceived that person with the scowl? Did it say this person is dark and ugly? This person is not a good person? This is a person I will not talk to or go near or recommend to my friends? What did you do with your will? Did you get up and leave? Did you turn away and move yourself out of that situation? What if that person needed to be accompanied, needed love?

Understand that the mind and emotion do not conclude around truth. They conclude around response that may be based on memory, protection, gain, and safety, on self in its separated identity. What if you had sat in that room and listened beyond mind and emotion and did not respond to will's decisions? If you had listened into the greater reaches of your being, the atmic centre, and had heard this being is sad, this being is scared, this being needs someone to be gentle, to give some compassion, perhaps then the scowl would not look like a scowl but would look like a down-turned countenance, and the grief that had looked black was just grief. Then the will could take your being closer and say, "Hello. How are you? How are you feeling?" In that moment of truth, in service, you have the ability to transform grief and fear, both within your being and reality and within theirs.

In responding from truth, beauty and freedom are created. The only way to respond from truth is to seek truth and hear it. The greatest source of truth is beyond mind, emotion, and body. It is in soul, the presence of eternal beingness that you are. That is who you are and that is who that person is who walked into the room. You are the same. What did you really want to leave when you wanted to leave the room? You wanted to leave your own self that was contracting with the fear of what that person was holding. You were walking away from yourself. You weren't walking away from another person. To respond in love and compassion is to merge with another being as self, to lift all the lower aspects of that being higher, into truth, as you have lifted your own.

Understand how to use mind, will, and emotion as servants of the higher presence of your being, the true identity of soul. As you learn to do this, you build a different reality. You transform the reality and belief systems that you are living within. You transform the patterns of protection, safety, and separation. Rather than moving away from other beings that are not exuding love and benefit to you, you move towards them. You merge with and give to them. You learn not to fear the human beings and situations around you. You learn to transform them. You learn what to believe and what not to. You begin to see the brittle emptiness of belief systems that the mind can so firmly create based on its emotions and the belief systems of others around you.

A passionate declarer of a truth that speaks with evangelical fervour will convince your mind - *this must be true.* Emotion can convince mind - dangerous ground. Beyond emotion is truth and peace. Peace exudes from truth. It is the aura, the Buddha-field of truth. Harmony is created from peace and unity is found.

Let your mind examine these things. Let it see two paths. Consider that there might be another path, perhaps every time, than the one it would most easily follow. The other path may have a very different set of beliefs within it, outcomes and actions. The mind likes to play with concepts. It delights in perception. Let the mind have the game of perception, then. Let it perceive the two paths that are always before it. One path holds that which is most right and the other path holds that which is less right. Consider the Buddhic teachings - right-thought leads to right-action, truth-filled thinking to truth-filled acting and feeling.

Where does the mind get its right, truth-filled thought? It will not get it from itself. The mind is a tool of the soul. The mind is a passing thing, a windowpane, just as the right hand is a passing thing, and the body - all that will burn. The eternal soul knows, accesses, and is of truth. As the mind realizes its place, reaches for *what is the right-thought here, what is the right-action*, it flows as swiftly as water down a channel and a right-thought is there. As the mind learns to cement its reality around this receiving of rightness, or truth, it becomes instantaneous. Right-thought occurs quicker and quicker and right-action simply follows.

As the mind learns to joyfully give way, to serve the master, the truth, it delights. It delights in its place, in the sense of rightness, the beauty and perceptions of right-thought. Likewise, the emotion delights in the feeling of truth and rightness. The harmonious principles that flow into the emotional being are delightful. Right-action is deeply fulfilling for it creates even more rightness out of itself. It creates bounty, fruition, love, embrace and unity.

There is no loss in going into right-thought and right-action. The body is at peace. There is no opposition of disruptive emotion, fear, and struggle, no contraction, anxiety, and tension running through the nervous system. The body is well. See the oneness, all the principles of beingness, and see that if these principles are lined up as servants and aspects of the atmic soul, truth is nurtured and manifested.

The mind must learn its place. It must be taught to reach for the higher thought, to listen for it. The will must be taught to act only on that which is felt and believed to be most true. And how is it to be assessed, what is true and what is not true? *Do not underestimate the human being.* The human being knows in the heart, in its depth, what is most true. If one were to sit in the stillness of prayer and meditation and listen beyond emotion and mind in its active struggling to declare, truth would be there.

*T*ruth is the wellspring, at the source of wealth for all human beings. What is most true creates unity, health, and expansion. It creates wellness and its ripples keep moving outwards, affecting every being and form in beneficial ways. This is the hallmark of truth.

The hallmark of untruth is that it creates disruption. It robs from the self, from the body, and as its ripples move outward, it increasingly robs, disrupts, contracts, and confines every being and form that it affects.

We ask, then, that you consider the tenets of mind to cement reality, to coalesce reality around what it perceives. Let be placed within the mind that which is most true, like a seed being planted, letting the mind repeat, if it will, the statements of that which is most true, letting the life rebuild itself around that. The momentum will gather. The life will shift and change and become stronger and more well. The relationships will become more peaceful and bounty will increase.

Belief

Behind right-action, right-speech, and right-thought is right-belief. One cannot speak, act, or think unless one believes. Belief is a sacred agreement to make. It is a tremendous power within consciousness, tremendous and dangerous. Belief is a marriage between that being and an entire reality. Ask yourself, "What am I marrying? What am I yielding my entire being to with the beliefs that I hold?" This is a sacred contract, and what you marry is what you shape.

We wish to speak about belief and about nurturing truth. This is a nebulous and vast question - what is to be believed in? For this reason, teachers have been given into the world, masters, demonstrators of truth. These awakened beings, these divine manifestations of truth, walk amongst humanity throughout time, giving you an image, perhaps a bank of teachings and stories, like a great seed of truth, to hold within your being. This is a way, then, to nurture and build truth, to let the mind find these teachings of the masters.

Who are the masters? Buddha, Christ, Krishna, Mohammed, Baha'u'llah, Krishnamurti, the high masters, the gurus — there are many, for the Divine Presence is generous and the human being is longing for itself, longing to exist in truth. Let the mind study, gather, and gain from the actions, stories, and words of these divinely given teachers. They are there as guidelines.

They demonstrate the highest atmic reality through form. They demonstrate the right use of mind, action, and will. They demonstrate the ultimate right use of form to divinely manifest and to manifest truth through form. They demonstrate this because this is who you are, this is what you are here for, and this is what you are learning every day, through everything that you do and every life you hold.

*All names
And forms are One*

*There are many races in this world
In different halls we pray*

*We call him by different names
The One who shows the way*

*The One who shows the way
My Lord, by what name
shall we pray?*

*Buddha, Krishna, Jesus, Allah,
Baha'u'llah, Sai Baba*

*Your children yearn to pray
You've come to show the way*

Devotional Bhajan

You will build and nurture truth more easily if you allow yourself to be taught by the lives, words, and actions of these beautiful beings. You do not need to take on their dogma or religion. You do not need to go shopping and choose. Listen to them all. Listen to the one who was given to you through your family line. Attach your being to the highest truth, to the demonstration of it, to the divine forms, the teachers. By attaching your being, you open to that line of information, that stream of reality.

The churches, the religious paths of the world – they are doorways to truth and humanity crowds them. You are right to question what humanity does with these pathways, and to question the belief systems that arise from these religions. Use your mind like a knife and cut through to what is true. What is that master really saying and being? Choose only that.

Realize also the power of the web that surrounds you. If the people around you are in devotion and sincerely seeking a right, true life, this web will lift you, penetrate you, and feed your mind, emotion, and will. Such is the power of spiritual community, of *sangha*. Such is the power of *darshan*, or being in the presence of one who has reached some level of attainment.

Realize the power of the web on mind, on the sacred contract of beliefs, yet never lose your choice. Realize the danger of the web, the belief systems that become cemented, that are destructive, in the name of the Christ or Buddha. Have discretion and individuality. And yet, if you have found the web of a spiritual community that feels pure and true, adopt it, move into it, sing the songs, enter the ceremonies. They infuse and fill your being with the patterns that lead you to truth, so that in the moment when the man with the different countenance enters the room, you find yourself entering into compassion first rather than judgment. Your being has been infused with a new reality, and the others in the room, your brethren, are doing the same!

We speak now of ways of building truth within mind, pathways between mind and soul, opening the being to itself and to its greatness. These ways are all around you, developing in pockets, here and there. The world is rich in ways to build the human being into its true nature. The world is broken open, the urn is spilled and the perfume is in the whole atmosphere. The teachings are no longer hidden. Nothing is unavailable, and you are here now.

The world now is as it has never been. The ways of India are here for you. The ways of Thailand, Tibet, China – it is all here. Develop a way, a practice whereby you repeatedly infuse your being with that which brings it into harmony, synchronicity, and leads it into sangha, a community where right-thought and higher realities are being studied and considered, where the intention is always towards truth.

Understand the ways of yoga. Yoga is a highway, a completeness, a bringing of awareness, action, and development to all aspects of the human being in order to create harmony, prowess, and attunement to the highest principles of soul and atmic truth. It is a practice and an action in the physical form that brings about openness and health within it. It is a focus on breath and life force, bringing awareness of them into the form, bridging form and consciousness through breath.

Yoga brings an awareness to the emotional being of humankind. One practices love, compassion, and devotion - devotion to a form of divine entity or avatar, through service, prayer, worship, and singing, devotion to truth, ultimately.

It is also a practice of bringing attention to mind - watching mind, knowing it, not being controlled or run by it, being aware of mind for what it is. It is meditation, a practice of consciousness – to watch mind and emotion and use them for what they are, to be freed of them.

Ultimately, yoga is a practice that brings harmony to all aspects of the human manifestation, so that the soul flows through all channels. To realize light-filled soul floods mind, heart, and form.

*T*he Buddhic practice of meditation, the eight-fold path, is another highway. It is there and available for you. It is the use of mindfulness to watch the physical form and know it for what it is, to not be bound by it, but use it in ways of rightness, to watch it as the vehicle that one exists within, and to know the separateness between the one who watches and the form one watches from. It is also to watch breath and life force, how life force infuses the physical form through breath, back and forth, creating a deeper, more expanded state of consciousness. See the power of breath in creating consciousness. This is mindfulness of breath.

The Buddhic way is to watch emotion and yet be outside of it, watching feelings come and go, watching what causes them to arise, and yet being outside of that, knowing that the one who watches is beyond feeling and only uses it.

The Buddhic path of mindfulness is a great path indeed, a powerful way of moving into true identity, no identity, the essence of Presence. The practice of meditation is one of gaining insight and absolute awareness into what mind, emotion, will, and physical form do, and ultimately settling into the expansiveness of Presence, the pure awareness of beingness, unbound to thought, name, or personality, to cause and effect, unbound by belief systems and what they cause. The Buddhic path leads to freedom. A Buddha is a freed being, no longer even bound to being called a being – freedom itself.

Wisdom has stilled their minds, and their thoughts, words, and deeds are filled with peace. Freed from illusion and from personal ties, they have renounced the world of appearance to find reality. They have reached the highest.

They make holy wherever they dwell, in village or forest, on land or at sea. With their senses at peace and minds full of joy, they make the forests holy.

The Dhammapada

The Christian path is a dear and sweet path, one of learning the principles of love. Jesus Christ was a teacher of love and compassion. He demonstrated in his life how to transform realities from constriction, separation, and fear into love, expansion, possibility, and grace. He taught that the human being is not to be bound to lifetime, form, restricted belief patterns, or judgment. He taught the human being that they are the essence of love. They are much more than their minds hold. He broke barriers of identity. He did this through dying, returning, and infusing all those that were receptive with his spirit, with the Great Counsellor.

> *Jesus said to them, " I am the way, and the truth, and the life; no one comes to the Father but by me. If you had known me, you would have known my Father also; henceforth you know him and have seen him.*
>
> *John 14.6*

Truly, truly, I say to you, he who believes in me will also do the works that I do; and greater works than these will he do, because I go to the Father. Whatever you ask in my name, I will do it, that the Father may be glorified in the Son; if you ask anything in my name, I will do it.

If you love me, you will keep my commandments. And I will pray the Father, and he will give you another Counsellor, to be with you forever, even the Spirit of truth, whom the world cannot receive, because it neither sees him nor knows him; you know him, for he dwells with you and will be in you.

John 14.12

𝓑uddha broke the barriers of the human being through emanating the presence and teachings of freedom, of being unbound. These beings are great jewels and gifts to you, each equally valuable. The Buddha – sublime, advanced, and mature teachings of how to build truth within the consciousness, a personal internal practice as with yoga, the lineage of Krishna and the Vedas. Christ – teachings of the heart, who to be in love with, to be in love only with God, in love with Love. Let these ways that are all around you be used. Sing the songs, enter the ceremonies that infuse your being and fill it with truth.

Currently in the world is the avatar Sathya Sai Baba, a great master of truth who gathers all who have come before him, who points in a circle to all. He points to truth through all forms that have come through, all paths and dogmas. He lifts truth to a new height, to a new teaching that frees it even further. He teaches the humanity of now, with a mind that has become so developed, with a consciousness that is ready to not carry myths or parables, delicate stories that walk around the core of truth. Sathya Sai Baba speaks and demonstrates directly the principles of truth that are so tremendous and brilliant they cannot be missed. He speaks all the words of truth that have ever been heard through any master before him, and gathers all diversity throughout all time into one.

Sathya Sai Baba teaches that to hold his form, his name, in the consciousness is to transform your being, to dissolve the past, the webs of untruth, and to bring about a direct linking to the soul. He teaches that by allowing your being to be filled with devotion for a master such as he, you dissolve all the structures within your being. As you let go and sing the name of God and hold the image of truth in a form that you recognize, a divinely infused human form, you enter the centre of the highway, the centre of the river where the flow is strong and direct and leads to the sea of expansion, the mergence with true nature.

He teaches that you are God. Do not seek God outside of you, for you will always be searching. You are God. Do not seek God in beings outside and beyond you. You are God. You are All. You contain the highest principles of truth and it is up to you to choose them and dissolve your structures of limitations and belief systems that pull you into separation. Then you have found God. God is nothing else.

Wherever you see, only God exists. Never doubt that God is here and not there. Wherever you search for him, He is there.

Telugu Poem

When you contemplate incessantly upon the Atma, you will see divinity everywhere. Hence, make efforts to recognize unity, realize it and become one with it. If you want to realize divinity, it is enough if you hold on to the principle of truth. Truth has a name and a form. Hold onto it firmly. Follow it implicitly. Only then will divinity reveal itself to you.

Everything is the Manifestation of God

Do not get deluded by names and forms. The youth of today lack steady mind because they are carried away by names and forms. Have firm faith that God is one, truth is one. Consider God as your sole refuge. Then wherever you go and whatever you see, you will find His manifestation. Wherever you see, He is there. He is not confined to one place. He is everywhere.

Sanathan Sarati
May 2004

*G*od is a pulsing, entire creation and non-creation of beingness. Every aspect of creation, every mineral, planet, fiery sun, or being – it is all God. The term 'God' says nothing. There is no word that can possibly gather the AUM. Aum is the sound and deeper meaning of all that is. The mind could never comprehend God. Outside of mind, in the atmic presence of beingness, God may be known, but only from within the very beingness of truth.

Masters are within the beingness of truth in absolute marriage and mergence. They speak, act, and exist from there and are not limited or dictated to by matter, mind, emotion, or self. They are not self! They are beyond all this. They speak from the freedom of true existence. Avatars can demonstrate this freedom through miracles - apparent manipulations of matter that we do not understand - the healing of bodies, people, and souls, the manifesting of objects out of thin air, the changing of events. They operate from the divine comprehension of reality, rather than a linear one. They use the same creative principles of mind and will as the human being, and yet are operating from beyond, from divine mind, divine will. These masters have a tremendous, vast message, teaching who we really are, who we have always been, that there is only a veil of unconsciousness that separates us. This veil carries belief systems that hold us bound and trapped in illusion and untruth.

Doors are unlocked, humanity! There are no more hidden teachings, no more hidden teachers in lofty monasteries for the few. The doors are unlocked. It is all there for you. There are many beings of awakened nature and immense capacity for teaching now. We needn't live in the confines and ignorance of mind-created reality any longer.

> *Ask, and it will be given you; seek, and you will find; knock, and it will be opened to you, for every one who asks receives, and he who seeks finds, and to him who knocks it will be opened.*
>
> Matthew 7.7

The Power Of Prayer, Meditation, Ceremony, & Ritual.

Prayer is a movement, an action within the consciousness, intention, and heart of an individual. It shows a commitment to learning, to living in truth, a desire to understand one's life in terms of truth and a higher order. Prayer is a lifting, a renewal, and a speaking within one's individual being towards this – how can I see this situation in its best light? How can I direct my life along the path of truth and light, as God would have it? How can I emulate my teacher, my lord, my master?

Prayer is an active time, a reviewing, learning, and opening towards the Great Counsellor, the source of wisdom and information that is God, through a chosen form, teacher, or avenue. Through aligning one's being to that teacher, one puts oneself in the place of reception and learning. Prayer is an action of reaching out for wisdom and understanding.

Prayer also needs to be understood as a time of receiving that very knowledge, for instruction to be received, direction and guidance to be given. Many go into prayer and end with the opening, the supplication, the commitment, but do not stay or believe in the receiving that can be immediate and direct. The human being largely does not understand its own consciousness and ability for reception of guidance and wisdom from the masters and from the great source. This reception, or answering of prayer, is looked for in the life that follows the prayer in a happening or an event, as though God were acting in that person's life according to that prayer.

Understand that being in prayer is placing oneself in alignment with truth. Through this, one's thoughts also are aligned. Therefore these events that follow a prayer are in alignment with truth, for it begins in the centre and moves outwards into manifestation. Through prayer one learns to listen and look for truth in the life, events, and interactions that follow the prayer. One chooses subtly or obviously the path that leads into experiences where truth speaks. Prayer is an alignment, a process. It is more than asking outside of oneself for intervention. It is an alignment with source, with truth, putting oneself into closer relationship with divine presence, divine action, and divine outcome.

Prayer is vital. Consider it. Consider the inner time that is provided in your days and use prayer correctly. There is not a great, unseen, nebulous being, a great benefactor who one applies to for one's needs to be met. There is rather an entire creation of which you are a part that is based on a foundation of love and which is evolving towards consciousness of love. This great creation, which is mentored, guided, and born of love, or God, is what you and all beings must learn to be merged with, absolutely conscious of, not separate from. Prayer is an action, and should be an action, of inviting divine truth and presence, into one's own thoughts and understandings as though saying, "I wish to be part of this. I wish to have this stream through my being and overcome all separateness. I wish to place myself in the river, be part of it. I wish to identify my life and being as sacred and part of Supreme Light."

In that alignment, then, Grace answers and speaks, for God is truth and love and the highest and lowest, the most articulate and most silent. God is within. Eternal Presence is what you are a part of, and through greater and greater alignment with truth, you and the events in your life become truth. Prayer, then, is a very direct and primary way of nurturing and building the true identity.

No matter what name or form you pray, 'tis but a means of finding the Supreme, who's all-pervading. May you grow aware of your true Self in him, Immaculate, and merge in THAT, Beatific Peace! For thus us perfect Realization found!

The Poems of Sri Ramana Maharshi

*M*editation is an action similar to prayer, and yet think of meditation as a moving into receptivity, a yielding openness to all that is. It is moving into pure consciousness of all that is, within and without, with no barriers or definitions of "within and without" – simply all-beingness. Meditation is a pure identification with truth, with the identity of truth within consciousness.

Prayer is a commitment and a striving to align one's being through thoughts, through communication inwardly to that place of All-beingness, the great presence of truth and love called God. Meditation is sitting, bathed in the absolute experience. Meditation is a state of consciousness that receives wisdom and the distinct understandings that are needed. Meditation moves one's being from emotion to vast peace, from a busy, engaged mind to a place of all-perceptiveness, receiving all. Meditation moves one's being from self to soul, from named being to the ever-nameless being, housing the consciousness of the all-nameless being, the presence of peace, within the body, brain, nervous system and breath.

Meditation is a primary action of a being wishing to move into truth and experience what it is, what the true identity of divine nature is. It is an action that moves the being that you are from mind to beyond mind, from emotion to peace, from personal identification to a mergence with All-being. Through daily or regular meditation, one infuses one's being, consciousness, and physical form with the energy of creation, with the nameless presence of God. This transforms every function within the body, mind, and emotional being. Slowly your being is transformed into one of consciousness, calm, equanimity, and health.

      From this foundation, one's life is met. One can understand what one's mind and emotions are to be used for. One can understand how to enter into the interactions of life and move directly through them, not getting washed over to an eddy, bound and spinning there in some emotional consequence or reaction, or some belief system that goes nowhere. One has found and infuses one's being with the true guide, the soul, the atma. Through that, all other faculties and aspects of the human being fall into place. They surround that central brilliance of light and truth and are utilized by it. Physical lifetime is an expression of truth. Meditation and prayer are primary actions to be used to transform one's being, to put oneself into attunement and alignment and transform one's character and relationship to life.

"I roused unflinching determination, focused my attention, made my body calm and motionless and my mind concentrated and one-pointed.

Standing apart from all selfish urges and all states of mind harmful to spiritual progress, I entered the first meditative state, where the mind, though not quite free from divided and diffuse thought, experiences lasting joy.

By putting an end to divided and diffuse thought, with my mind stilled in one-pointed absorption, I entered the second meditative state quite free from any wave of thought, and experienced the lasting joy of the unitive state.

As that joy became more intense and pure, I entered the third meditative state, becoming conscious in the very depths if the unconscious. Even my body was flooded with that joy of which the noble ones say, "They live in a binding joy, who have stilled the mind and are fully awake.

Then, going beyond the duality of pleasure and pain and the whole field of memory-making forces in the mind, I dwelt at last in the fourth meditative sate, utterly beyond reach of thought, in that realm of complete purity, which can be reached only through detachment and contemplation.

This was my first successful breaking forth, like a chick breaking out of its shell...."

Someone once asked the Buddha sceptically, "What have you gained through meditation?"

The Buddha replied, "Nothing at all."

"Then, Blessed One, what good is it?"

"Let me tell you what I lost through meditation: sickness, anger, depression, insecurity, the burden of old age, the fear of death. That is the good of meditation, which leads to nirvana."

The Dhammapada

Ceremony

*P*urely speaking, ceremony is a group or individual action that serves to bring about alignment and attunement to truth. Prayer, then, is a ceremony in a very simple and pure way. Ceremony is a learned and developed action that signals the consciousness, emotion, will, intention, and the entire being to be in that alignment, to open up to the attunement of God, Divine presence, Grace.

Ceremony has become greatly elaborate. The human being does this, has needed ceremony, needed the trappings, clothing, smells, sounds, and sights of ritual and ceremony. All these appeal to the senses – the incense, candles, chanting, hymns, robes, churches - they are all creations of the human being that is striving for truth and alignment with love, grace, and blessing. Honour and delight in what the human being does in ceremony. It is the soul reaching for itself.

Ceremony is a place of purification and consecration where the human being is trying to reflect, review, and lift his or her own actions to a higher place, to commit his or her life along a higher road that moves more swiftly and directly to peace. Trust ceremony. If it is being used purely, it is powerful, for the human senses are overcome with the sights, sounds and smells of ritual. The soul is invited forward into consciousness. The artist that the human soul is strives to make beautiful what is being seen and heard, strives to bring the soul forward to experience the beauty of truth.

How many in the world do not trust ceremony and put it aside, living in bare moments, not having ceremony or ritual to invite them forward? This too is to be respected and understood for ceremony has become dead and a bondage, caught in sights, smells, sounds, words, and actions without allowing and realizing any longer what they are meant for. The human being is easily caught in repetitive patterns, in the familiar, forgetting what the very pattern is for, not realizing why it needs to change. Perhaps in the middle of the ceremony, there is the need to sit and receive a revelation or an understanding, to sit bathed in pure presence, and it is not allowed for the ceremony itself is not finished. Ceremony should not be rigid and fixed. It is meant to lift the human being further into alignment and attunement and as each individual within the ceremony moves in that direction, they will have a different response, a different gift and offering.

Ceremony has also stayed in the realm of emotion, getting caught in passion and fervour in the emotional being. Peace, atmic consciousness, is beyond emotion. Joy and love can be felt as emotions, but these are also great spreads of conscious light, bringing stillness and freedom beyond emotional expression. Emotion is to be respected and allowed but not stayed with. Gratitude and joy may pass through the heart. It is a movement like the passage of music. It is a bathing in great presence. Emotion is not to be sought for as the end result of ceremony. Rather, it is a passage where one's being recognizes they are coming close to the sun, to the brilliant heart of beauty.

Ceremony is meant to lead the being into a pure understanding of all-beingness, beyond self and separation. It is meant as a baptismal bath in pure spirit. Can one get put into the baptismal water and just end up wet? It would be best not to use the ceremony of water if it deflects from the experience of immersion into truth. Do not get caught in the baptismal waters, in the rituals, the ceremonies that are simply symbolic of the real thing. Use ceremony lightly, with respect, like the paintbrush of an artist. The image, the artistry, sits purely within. The paintbrush is a tool to express that and bring one's consciousness closer to the beauty that is being experienced within.

Ceremony and ritual are especially helpful as a way to focus a group into divine alignment, very useful when one is struggling on one's own and unable to come into that immersion alone. A group pooling their intentions together magnifies them and assists everyone. "When two or more pray in my name, I am there." When two or more gather together in the name of truth, truth is magnified. Realize this dynamic of praying, meditating, and creating ceremonies together. Trust it, keeping your clear and conscious eye on the dangers of bondage, of repetitive action that leads nowhere, of ceremony that has gathered dust and needs change. But do not disregard ceremony itself.

Consider creating ceremony. Consider letting it arise out of your life and your group. Let it be fresh and new – a new picture being painted. Let ceremony reflect what is truth and the need for truth now. Let this come into your churches and circles, the newness and ever-changing nature of the evolving human being, using ceremony and yet letting it be refreshed. Let it grow. Listen to the individuals within the group, what comes from each one. Let ceremony be a production of more than one leader. Let it arise from the group. Let it be dynamic and alive and real as it is happening.

Ceremony is a learning process for the mind, emotion, and will, to learn how to place themselves under the guidance of soul. Do not disregard the ways of old, and the greatness of the human being in ceremony and ritual. Let your choice be 'yes' to the essence of this, and 'no' to bondage and restriction.

Realize also that if your being strives to be in alignment and truth, you could enter into any ceremony. Let it carry you there. You did not need the ceremony, and did not need to care how it was created around you. You entered into the stream of its intention and you arrived. Therefore you, Freed-One, can go into any church or any temple and find God. God is universal; God is All-beingness and God's truth is universal. The human being is a unity of oneness in truth and God. You, Freed-One, neither need ceremony nor ritual nor church nor temple, yet can delight in and embrace any ritual, any church, and any temple. You can bring love and presence into any place and add to it and need not judge or criticize any place or action in these ways.

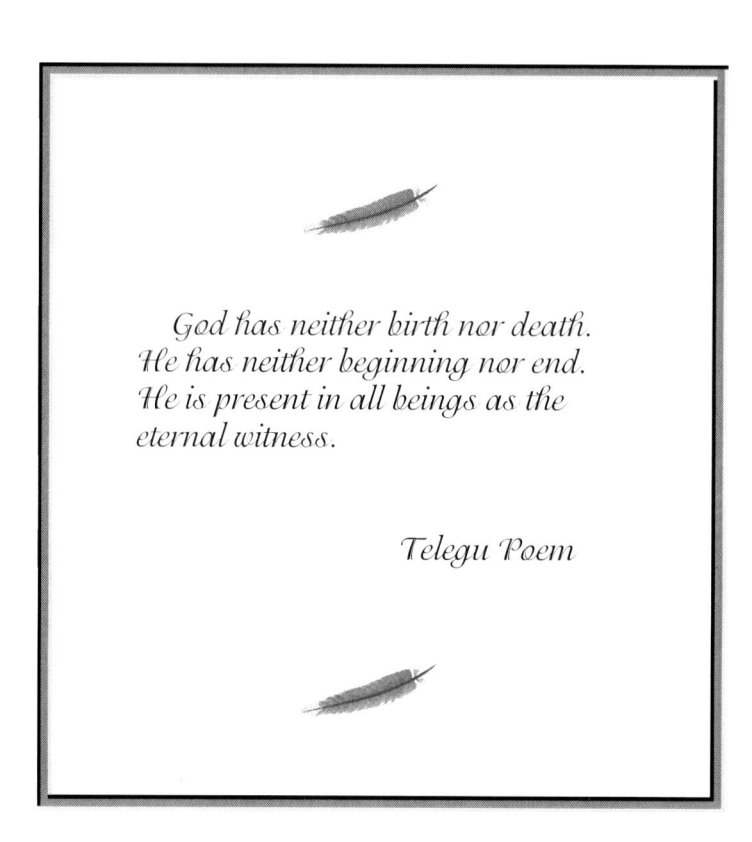

*God has neither birth nor death.
He has neither beginning nor end.
He is present in all beings as the
eternal witness.*

Telegu Poem

Speaking, then, on the ways to build and nurture truth, we point directly to the ways of old, of prayer, meditation, and ceremony. We point to them unerringly and say *yes*. Yes, but let it be alive and dynamic and true. Yes, yet do not be dependent on outward rituals, ceremonies, organizations, groups, or religions. Match them with your own inner ceremonies and actions of commitment. You may name yourself a Buddhist, Hindu, or Christian, may join a Vipassna or Zen meditation group, or Christian prayer group. Do all this and yet go beyond the name, path, and weekly date, for otherwise you will not enter. It must be your own, and your meditation must lead to a place where it is no longer Zen or Vipassna or prayer, or whatever term anyone has given. Your state of peace must be arrived at without being in the name of Jesus Christ, Lord Buddha, or Sathya Sai Baba. It must be beyond name, forms, and paths. It must be a pure experience of love, peace, and enlightenment. Then one can step back in great gratitude and devotion to the form, path, teacher, and lord.

       Buddha said that his teachings are a raft, and yet not to stay on it, but let it carry you across to the new soil of freedom. A master, religion, ritual, or ceremony – these are all rafts, passages, and actions that lead you into the greatness of truth. Rafts are necessary. They were developed and designed by the higher nature to lead the lower nature to it. Find and accept your raft, and be on it with your whole body. When it leads you to the other shore, get off the raft and be there.

Whom the Muslims adore as Allah, whom the Christians adore as Jehovah, whom the Varshnava adore as Phulabia, whom the Saivites adore as Sambhu, who grants in answer to their prayers health, long life, prosperity, and happiness to all, wherever they may be, He, the One God, is the God of all mankind. God is one and only one.

      Sathya Sai Baba

Devotional Music

We will speak now on singing, chanting, bhajans, hymns, and using music as a raft and a way to build and grow into divine identity.

Understand music, how it overtakes the entire being on a great pulse and wave directly into what it is saying, not with words alone but with tones, with cants. Music bypasses mind, as is well known. Music disregards mind and communicates deeply into the body, into emotion. Music moves beyond the boundaries and barriers of separation. It is a great vehicle, a great strong raft.

We are taught to use devotional bhajans as a way of going into attunement and alignment, such as one would use meditation. Use the repeated singing of devotional phrases to sink their meanings into the consciousness and to act as seeds that will grow in one's actions, thoughts, and feelings. It brings groups of people together into the magnified experience of alignment and immersion in higher thought and truth. This way is well known and has been used for eras and eras of human development. Use music consciously as a form to nurture your being forward, as a format for your ceremony and groups. Try it and experience it.

Music should be simple and repetitive so as to bypass mind. The mind says, "Why am I doing this over and over? I've already said this. Why am I saying this phrase ten more times?" And then after a time the mind lets go. A phrase of beauty can be said a thousand times. Need there be an end to it? The mind is what would qualify that phrase and say, "It should begin here, and once said it is said." Beauty has no beginning, ending, or qualification. A repeated phrase of truth can lift a being into the experience of that truth and immerse one's entire life in it, even when it is not being sung.

 Music is a powerful vehicle unlike any other. It arrives in and pleases the senses, vibrates the cells, enters every organ, involves the breath, stills the mind, and involves the entire physical form. Music is not simply a singing of words together. It is a form of committing oneself through entering into the joyousness and experience. Music is an expression of joy, love, devotion, and service. But it can be destructive, for it is also an expression of anything that the human being holds within. So we are speaking of devotional music that lifts one to realization and joy.

 Consider what music you listen to, sing, or play. What is it committed to and what is it building in your consciousness? What are the blues doing to the singer or listener? What truth is being imprinted and cemented into that being through the music they listen to? Listen to the radio and think of that. What reality is being repeatedly painted by that music? What is sinking into the cells, the energy field, and the core of the listener or singer? Therefore choose music in this light, listening to what is there and considering, "Do I wish to be immersed in this reality?"

Music is an immersion. Music is resonant to the human being in all stages of consciousness. It is a universal raft or method of creating truth and developing alignment. Music can lift one who is an infant in form or consciousness. It can lift a disabled, handicapped, or conscious individual. It reaches everyone, every creature and form of matter. It is an activated energy form that penetrates all matter.

Music, then, is a powerful tool. It can lift matter into a finer expression of itself. It can create more developed and perfect cell division and more attuned responsiveness to the information being replicated. Music brings consciousness to cell division and to all forms. It stimulates growth to be more conscious and penetrates truth-filled consciousness into the physical matter. Music in pregnancy is a tool that brings nurturance and finer development to an infant. It is a healing tool for cell and organ repair. It encourages the vital force to exist more fully within its form. Music encourages the embodiment of form, inviting the soul forward through its body, its healing process, and its birth.

Music can also be destructive. Music that expresses anger, hatred, depression, and great sadness, or that has no harmony, or has counter harmonies that go against each other, sound levels that confuse - this music will also affect physical cell growth. Music can put stillness into cell division, or activate it to a point of confusion. This is the same truth about disharmonious sound of any form.

We call music 'organized sound', other sound being 'disorganized sound'. Organized sound is placed together with an intention and carries the meaning and energy of that intention. Therefore music is powerful sound. You who are seeking freedom – use music and sound accordingly.

Service

*T*his next section is on ways to build and nurture the soul and consciousness of truth.

Service has been taught through all religions and masters. It is the way for an individual to break out of a separate sense of self and isolation into a realization of unity, of the sameness and oneness of all beings. To bring happiness to another is to bring happiness to the whole and to the giver. To bring comfort, food, nurturing compassion, and assistance to any other being brings it to all beings because they are essentially one being. It brings it to the giver who is also enjoined with all beings.

Consider the golden rule – do unto others as you would have them do unto you. What is this really saying? It speaks of the law of unity, the truth of oneness of all beings, that outer actions create one's inner truth and state of being. By serving and acting in love outwardly, one exists and lives in love inwardly. By breaking the separation, one lives in the wholeness of beings. By identifying with others as God, one can learn to identify within oneself as God.

True service, then, is bringing all the words and aspects of God, love, truth, and grace to every being that is before you, whether they appear deserving or not, beautiful or not, receptive or not, calling each one of those beings you – that is me, we are one. Where the need lies the strongest is where it is most difficult to say, "That is me and this is where the service needs to go."

In the true nature of service there is this humble identifying with all-beingness. There is not the one with plenty and the one with naught, the one of lofty, superior riches, whether financially or spiritually, and the one devoid of such things. Therefore the beggar that you are giving to is not less than you, for you are the beggar. You may have had a life of doing that very action. You may have had an emotion yesterday that felt just like that. Identify with all you see as one being and give into it. By giving to the beggar, you lift beggary from your own being; you give into your own being and teach it the abundance, plenty, and love that it needs to hear.

Service is a direct path to develop pure, true consciousness of divine nature. It is a karma path, an action path, and one that places you on the streets, in the offices, in the schools. It places you in the midst of humanity and it exercises your knowledge, meditations, prayers, and wisdom. Your identity as divine nature becomes stronger. You do not become separate or lofty; you become part of. You appreciate all aspects of creation. If you look long enough, you might see that being whom you judged doing an act of grace; you may see him awed by a flower; you may watch tears of compassion come to his eyes as he watches a child learning to ride a bike. Did you look long enough to see who he was? He was you! Have you ever felt like that, like just wanting to die, not wanting to try? Have you ever felt like nothing and nobody, with no reason to exist? That is you.

One in service becomes aware of humanity as self and serves the whole in that light, not thinking of personal gain, but of the entire human being's gain of which he or she is a part. There is great gain in service, for the happiness you create in another becomes your own. The freedom you create in another and the realization of All-beingness becomes your own.

Service is a great and strong path to choose and is the sign of a maturing consciousness, of a true adult. Parenting is a tremendous tool in evolution. A parent is forced to learn service. And yet, we are not speaking of a forced expectation into service but a conscious choice that moves beyond parenting into the community, into the other children that do not tug your heartstrings, who are not beautiful or of your own creation, moving beyond that which is expected of you to that which is not expected, beyond the call of duty to a choice of service.

When you see others in such service, honour them. Learn from them. They are teachers for you. They are great ones. Recognize those who are in service and help them. Let them show you the way.

And a ruler asked him, "Good Teacher, what shall I do to inherit eternal life?" And Jesus said to him, "Why do you call me good? No one is good but God alone. You know the commandments: "Do not commit adultery, Do not kill, Do not steal, Do not bear false witness, Honour your mother and father. And he said, "All these I have observed from my youth." And when Jesus heard it, he said to him, "One thing you still lack. Sell all that you have and distribute to the poor, and you will have treasure in heaven; and come, follow me. But when he heard this he became sad, for he was very rich. Jesus looking at him said, "How hard it is for those who have riches to enter the kingdom of God! For it is easier for a camel to go through the eye of a needle than for a rich man to enter the kingdom of God. Those who heard it said, "Then who can be saved?" But he said, "What is impossible with men is possible with God.

Luke 18.18

Devotion

What is devotion? Devotion is service. It is aligning and attuning oneself. Devotion is behind the singer's intention and the guitar player's hands. We have been speaking of devotion all along, and yet now we speak of it directly. Devotion is a state of the heart. It is an action or intention of the being to place oneself as a student, child, devotee, and disciple at the feet of a teacher, an example of divine nature and ultimate beauty. Those who can understand and choose devotion have stepped into the middle of the river where the current is the strongest and will arrive swiftly at the nirvana sea, the actual and total experience of truth.

Why? How does devotion do this? Devotion uses the emotional being, the emotional centre of the human consciousness, which is powerful in itself. A human being in hatred and anger destroys life, destroys selves, interferes with cell divisions and creates destruction. A human being in love, not lust but *love*, speeds the growth of a plant towards its flower, brings about a wholeness and completeness in cell division, an expansion and higher realization to children, events, and life. A human being using their emotional centre in love sits at the very core of creation and emanates outward through all its forms, bringing about harmony and alignment.

The mind could never do this. The mind could consider beauty, grace, and truth until the cows come home. But the heart understands and sits at the centre in the most transformative position - to transform creation and place one's being into alignment.

Therefore devotion is an action of using the heart fully. Then the human being moves beyond, "I live for myself, I live as this named person", into "I live for you, for all. I prostrate myself at the feet of all beings." Through absolute prostration one gives up one's individual, isolated, confined self and moves into the truth of beingness. That master whose feet you kiss is a passing form of divine presence. Those finite feet you kiss walk a path into infinity. Through aligning oneself with the form of a master, one enters through the doorway most surely, most accompanied, and in a high agreement to be embraced, infused, and transformed into a being such as the one being followed.

Jesus Christ's words - *I am the way, the truth. No one enters into the Father but by me.* What did he mean? Are these controversial words meant to exclude all other religions, masters, and avatars, other great examples and forms of divine beingness? No. They are meant to say, "Through devotion to my being, life, example, and words, you will become this truth. You will be embraced and merged to the Father, the source."

Sathya Sai Baba speaks – if you hold incessantly my form in your consciousness and heart, you will enter into the experience of the divine; you will leave your karmic past behind, be cleansed, and renewed. By always holding the name of God on the lips, in the heart and mind, one transforms into a being of God. Devotion, then, is a direct path to becoming truth.

And yet devotion is not understood or trusted in the West. It has appeared harmful, as though it takes choice away. Blind devotion is not what we speak of. We speak of conscious devotion. We do not speak of tradition, ritual, and expectations. We do not speak of those forms of devotion whereby the source, the master, the teacher is not being questioned. Blind devotion leads to blindness; conscious devotion leads to consciousness.

Again, let it be fresh and new. If it is the Lord Jesus Christ, then let it be the truth of the Lord Jesus Christ, not the rituals or interpretations. Let it be the truth of the master that you devote yourself to, the living form, actions, words, and presence, and realize that the avatar you choose and attune yourself to is a brilliant doorway that opens wide and lovingly for you. As you pass through the lintel of that brilliant doorway, the master dissolves into the light, for that's all he ever was. Then you, too, are surrounded by the very light that was in the words, face, feet, and actions of that master.

The master stands in the doorway, beckoning you, and until you come right up to those feet and to that doorway, he appears as he does. But as you devote yourself entirely and kiss the feet and attend to that master's truth incessantly within your being, the master dissolves into the light and carries you through the doorway. Where are you then? You are in the peace and freedom of divine beingness. You are the truth of divine beingness. The master and all masters surround you.

      Listen to the meaning of devotion and consider it. Listen to these ways of devotion we speak of. If you can reach out and allow yourself to have a divine example, a guru, an avatar, a swami, then you make swifter your journey to and through the brilliant doorway.

The Brilliant Doorways

This is a teaching into avatars, or divine masters.

There is no more worthy place to put one's attention and education as to this: to understand, point the awareness, and open the consciousness to these beings that have been given to humanity cyclically throughout time; to let one's mind and eyes look to these teachers, to what they said, how they lived and demonstrated; to listen deeply into what they said and watch how they lived; to understand what was not said, what could not be heard clearly at that time, watching purely their example. These beings exist in a full consciousness without lapse. Every act, every word, every event in their lives is teaching, is written in the soul of all humanity. Every story that is carried on through dogma or religion is meant to be there - a seed story, a parable of great potency. There is no more worthy place to point one's attention.

Why would this be said? There is nothing loftier, nothing higher than the human being realizing fully who it is. There is no study so encompassing as the study of these divine teachers. All other study is on the aspects and dynamics of creation. To examine the lives and teachings of an avatar is to investigate the essential core of creation itself, to study the source of one's own being and the reality of All-being. It is the greatest text in the library, the text that includes all. There is none more intelligent or more skilled than an avatar - an omniscient, all-knowing being. All physics, all math, all language, all art, all aspects of creation are present in perfection. We are not saying do not study the aspects of creation, the math, the sciences, the arts. Rather, place one's primary focus towards the ultimate study of truth as is shown through the avatars, or the divine manifestation of Supreme Beingness.

Who are the avatars? Who are the divine manifestations that have come into humanity throughout time? There are those known and those not known. Those known to the present mind are those whom the religions have been founded upon. Each of these founders, so to speak, is of a different quality, purpose and completeness of divine manifestation. Yet all speak of, point to, and demonstrate the essential truth in their lives.

Humanity has the words, the life, the parables, and the teachings of Jesus Christ, Gautama Buddha, Lord Krishna, Ramana Maharshi, Sathya Sai Baba, Babaji, and Mohammed. All great teachers, all meaningful, purposed manifestations of God.

The story of truth can be understood best if all teachers are listened to. India, the land of Bharat, the sacred, spiritual heart of humanity, is continually manifesting divinely realized beings, some quietly, some visibly. There are many lineages of teaching pathways in India. India stands apart in its richness of divine manifestations. Most avatars throughout time have originated if not passed through India. It is to be held as a treasure in the human consciousness, to be turned to as the rich wealth, the library of truth.

What are avatars? What are they like? How do we find them? An avatar is a truly realized being in full consciousness of supreme Beingness, beyond the laws of matter and physical form, and beyond the grasp of human self, emotion, will and mind. Such a being is fully operating on the divine principles of all-knowing. Such a being is in the place of creator, rather than created, and is completely conscious of the origination of all matter, all forms and all situations involving form. An avatar is not subject to creation and yet is master of creation. This means, then, that an avatar can create, change and manipulate matter, heal illness, and change the course of a being's life and their karma, changing the sequence of events.

Humanity calls these miracles. "Miracle" to the human mind means that which goes beyond comprehension, beyond the laws of matter, cause and effect. Really what the human being is saying is that it doesn't understand. Truly, it cannot comprehend what is happening. The human being is bound to the laws of matter, cause and effect, karma, and unconsciousness. Avatars are masters of these laws and use them to teach and demonstrate existence beyond unconsciousness, beyond bondage. They are teaching that this is our capacity, the capacity of consciousness itself, which the human being is developing.

The human being is on a slow and steady path to realizing greater and greater consciousness and capacity. Yet it is still a long way from moving through the veil of ignorance and illusion to realizing there is only one great unity of absolute consciousness and one's existence is not defined or dictated by form. Rather, form is subject to consciousness. Therefore, if the avatar, such as Sai Baba, sees fit to create a golden ring for a devotee, that golden ring appears in an instant in his palm. This occurs daily in the life of this avatar, manifesting matter with purport and reason for his devotees.

    The Lord Jesus Christ was also in a state of being to master matter, to create healing, to create bread and wine and a physical form once his human one had been crucified. A being of supreme consciousness can create the human form at will, when it is needed, only doing so in order to teach. Death is no obstacle. Death is simply the ceasing of the gross physical body. The physical form can be manifested from the essential conscious place of being, which is beyond the laws of form, into a higher dynamic of laws of supreme consciousness. The physical form can then be manifested around a purpose. This is done often in India. It has been done often throughout time.

    To the western mind it has not been shown, except for in the story of Jesus Christ. Listen and watch this great story - the great teachings of this man of Israel, Issa, beyond what his words said to the people at that time, who could only comprehend so much. Watch him. Watch how death did not take him. Watch how he demonstrated the laws of supreme consciousness. He showed you who you are; he showed you the meaning of being free; he showed you the way - love one another. He showed you the steps to exist in ultimate freedom from suffering.

Listen and watch the words and life of the Buddha, who also spoke of the ultimate freedom, of letting go of the illusion of self and separateness and moving into the absolute consciousness that can no longer be called self.

Listen to the teachings of the diamond sutra that a rose is not a rose. A rose is composed of the elements of all creation and is lightly, temporarily shaped into the form it is in. Do not see a rose just as a rose. See it as all. See it as yourself. Look beyond the forms around you and do not be fixed and bound by what you see. Realize that in the greater conscious state all is flowing and streaming, composed of the same elements, coming from and streaming towards the same source. Buddha sees the rose as a miracle. Listen to the joy of that freedom that does not see the rose as a series of petals fixed to a stem but as a miracle.

Each brilliant doorway, each teacher of divine wisdom, teaches a different aspect of the same truth at a different time in humanity to a different mind and level of consciousness. The picture becomes clear when you listen to them all, allowing the separation between the ways, the dogmas, to dissolve. Let go of all that has been created in the name of religion and just listen to the purest words and teachings, watching the life and what it demonstrated.

Mohammed - his beautiful, powerful, essential teaching. Though he was not an avatar, he was a teacher, a prophet-channel of God. Understand there are gradations of such, that the person sitting beside you is also visited by truth and teaching you. Understand there are those beings that are absolute divine manifestations of omniscience and are operating beyond the laws of matter and form, and there are those that are prophets, teachers, visited by great realization and revelation, but not divinely, fully-realized avatars. Mohammed was directed from his soul to unify the consciousness of humanity into a beautiful, spiralling, one-pointed awareness. He was demonstrating and teaching unity, bringing together the many forms and faces of God into one. We hold here the image of the mosque, with its domed, beautiful spiral against the sky, ending in a single point in the light - one God. Listen to this powerful, essential teaching. If you were to understand it in its context, you would respect and fit it into the speaking and teaching that comes from all religions.

  Humanity can be scattered into looking for God in many forms. It can become superstitious, thinking God exists in the form of an idol or a sequence of events. It can believe that there is this or that God, this group believing in that one and that group believing in another. In short, the human mind can become scattered, still with its same desire for truth through deity, and yet deity becoming multiple, fragmented, and causing division within peoples. Mohammed was directed in the soul to point at a oneness of God, to bring and lift the human consciousness from its fragmentation to a stronger foothold, developing the ability to realize that there is just one creator, thereby strengthening the weakened humanity and ending the divisions that further weaken it. Mosques are a great symbol of this strength, a great gesture of lifting the consciousness.

Religions, or what humanity does with the teachings it is given, are another story. Therefore, listen purely to the original teaching, if it can be found. Often, the esoteric and mystical forms of a teaching are where the truth can be heard more directly.

Listen to the Sufis. They understand mergence with God consciousness. They learn to let the multiplicity, the aspects of reality, spin, until there is only one presence, pulsing and streaming in.

Listen to the Essenes, the mystic roots of Issa. They learned to remove their consciousness from the grasp of self, body, and culture and move into a pure understanding of what the Christ was saying.

At present in this century is a tremendous gift in the story and life of Sathya Sai Baba. He has a high teaching of unity, bringing all religious understanding to a new point of unity, a universal teaching of truth and a very active, dynamic demonstration of supreme Beingness. He teaches that it is unnecessary to crowd the planes to India to be at his feet. He is everywhere. He is beyond form and beyond India. The human being must not idolize, not place images on his altar, but realize within one's own being the truth and capacity of love and consciousness. The teachings of all these beings throughout time and at present stream and waft around the world like an urn of perfume shattered. The teachings of the Dalai Lama are everywhere. The teachings of the Thich Nat Han are everywhere. Buddha teaches a thousand-fold. Jesus Christ teaches a thousand-fold, through many beings and faces. They are all one being. You need go no farther than your breath or a bookstore to find the teachings of divine truth.

When we speak of Sathya Sai Baba, we say that this time of humanity is significant and powerful. A teacher of great omniscience exists in the form, emanates the truth of divine wisdom and reality within our midst like a leaven within the dough that is active. Rejoice and know this. Visitation of divine Beingness to humanity is a great gift, a great moment, and it is here again, not only through the form of Sathya Sai Baba, but appearing as light in many beings of greatness. The brilliance is greater than the sun.

Sri Ramana Maharshi is a most beautiful divine example of beingness from this last century. His simple, profound life of beaming absolute love silently into the souls of his devotees has given humanity another jewel on its prayer bead string. Ramana's teaching and life story are available to all and have a uniqueness of nakedness and simplicity to the "truth of being". There is no religion around his name or being, no volumes of texts or interpretations. Ramana Maharshi 'just is the absolute presence' simply gazing upon us.

Baha'u'llah, who has become the founder of the Baha'i faith, is also a great teacher of the unity of consciousness, the unity of all beings. He was directed towards oneness, towards lifting and freeing the humanity from fragmentation and division. And yet now, as you hear of these things, the Baha'i, the Hindu, the Islamic, the Christian, what do you hear? Do you hear and observe division or unity? Indeed you observe division.

Humanity strays quickly from the source of the teaching to interpretation, trying to create safety, home, familiarity and ownership. The teachings themselves - of compassion, grace, forgiveness, and nurturing all humanity as though it were your own - would dissolve such things. So what you observe is the state of the human being, not the essence of the teachers. A great being it is that can embrace all faiths and yet be beyond them, celebrating and calling as teacher all those who have been given but claiming none for itself.

Brilliant doorways are there with different forms appearing, standing there for a lifetime, and dissolving back into the light. They are beckoning you to come, not only to lay your alms before the doorway and then return to where you came from, but to come to the doorway and step through, allowing your form, bondage, and limitations to dissolve as well. Your religion is before the doorway; freedom is after the doorway.

So-called founders of religions are never on this side of the doorway. They did not say, "Create a religion." They beckoned humanity through the door and humanity created great structural pathways that lead to the door and away again, never passing through.

Now Sathya Sai Baba stands there, holding a sign, the symbol of all religions throughout all times surrounding a pillar of truth that says: Do not bother creating any more religion; do not bother creating any more elaborate structures that come and go from this door. Pass through this doorway. Dissolve your illusions of pain, suffering, limitation, and ignorance. Receive the true education once and for all.

*There are many races
in this world.
In different halls we pray.*

*We call him
by different names
the one who shows the way.*

*The one who shows
the way, my Lord,
By what name shall we pray?*

*Krishna, Buddha,
Jesus, Allah,
Baha'u'llah, Sai Baba*

*Your children long to pray
You've come to show the way*

Bhajan Song

Foundations of the Future

We ask the Guidance to teach on Karma, the process of human lives and how karma operates. The focus of this is to counsel and encourage patience and understanding towards the process of karma, and how it is to be used and understood.

Karma - The Journey of a Potter

We show fingers shaping clay. We show the carefulness and knowledge of a potter in shaping the clay pot. What is built into that wet clay, indeed that very quality of the clay, determines the strength of that pot once it's gone through its drying, its firing and its usage. Therefore in the stages of the pot, the quality of the clay is a primary stage. Knowledge and skill of the shaping and drying of clay and the firing of the pot - all determine the capacity of the usage, the longevity and usefulness. Through this image of the pot, clay and potter, one can see the dynamics of karma. Every life, every event within your life, has this quality of clay.

The clay - what is being chosen to build your days, consciousness and reality with? What conditions, relationships, thoughts and endeavours you choose, what you put your energy into, how you feed your body, mind, and soul, determines the quality of the clay that you are shaping your life with.

  The shaping of the pot, the skill of the fingers, the knowledge of how thick and what shape to make the pot - what foresight does the potter have for how this pot should be used and what is needed? Does he create a pot that has no capacity for use or does he shape one that has great capacity? The knowledge of the potter based on memory, reflection, openness to teachers who came before, learning from failed pots, and being attentive to humanity and what is needed - all goes into the shaping of that pot and the knowledge of how to create a structure that will serve its purpose.

  This, then, is likened to how one is throughout their day. How does one work with relationships and situations? How does one work within their field, with what knowledge, with what foresight? Thinking of what humanity needs, learning from the teachers and experiences that one has had, all go into the shaping of that day and situation. In short, what do you bring into your day? What do you bring into your course of study or work or family? Do you bring foresight of what needs to be created? Do you bring hindsight of what hasn't worked for many others, or for you, and what to avoid? This is your skill as the shaper of your reality and your future.

  Once you have set a shape in your being with your personality, character, life choices and reality, it is there, it is built. It goes through its trials, its firing. Life experiences are this firing. As your children grow into their maturing years, they try you; they try out the values that you have implanted in them, because the work you've created moves forward and tries what you have placed into it and how you are maintaining it. How will your creation hold in the fire of challenge? Much of life is about that - a firing of what you have set in motion and created, of belief structures and inner reality.

This is the meaning of karma. What has been created is being lived in and tried. Does it stand true or does it shatter and crack in the fire of life experience? Once it has been fired, is it intact? Can it bear fruit, hold water and be used, or is it simply a useless, cracking, aging structure? How does this look in human terms? Have your children created lives that continue to grow and evolve in consciousness and freedom, or are your children struggling as adults, with alcohol, unconsciousness and dysfunction? Has the work that you were in and developed continued? Is it dynamically growing and becoming wider and more fruitful, or has it gone into bankruptcy and disintegration because it was not built on the right values and could not deal with the fire of life experience? This is karma.

Karma is not a great god sitting above you on a throne giving a sentence. Karma is simply the result of your own creation. It is the law of cause and effect, there to evolve a being into greater consciousness. It is a law of this dimension, of forms and evolving consciousness. Unconscious actions create greater unconsciousness. Conscious actions create greater consciousness. Any action done in protection, hatred, greed, contraction, negativity and ill will create results based on the same. Any action or creation based in love, expansion, and compassion will create the same. And so does the law of karma go that the creation deepens and expands as it moves on, so therefore that which is created in unconsciousness creates a greater unconsciousness, and that which is created in consciousness creates greater consciousness.

This teaches all forms - the human being and the animal and plant worlds - to develop in greater and greater ability and capacity in consciousness. Use this law with more and more awareness. Consider what you're doing. Realize that what you do in this time and day is working with the beginning stages of clay that will later become the pot. It may not even be in this life. It may be in what is yet to come. What you create now is the structure of tomorrow. That is where your awareness should truly go. Use your hope, optimism and learning in that way, so that what you do today creates beauty, fruitfulness and expansion tomorrow.

As to what has been created yesterday and has resulted in today: be aware; be conscious; be reflective. Be compassionate towards unconsciousness in yourself and others and be committed to consciousness. To be regretful, hateful or critical towards unconsciousness will only create more unconsciousness. Guilt and shame should only be fleeting realizations of what unconsciousness has created.

Compassion should then be given instead. Say to one's self, "Through my great unconsciousness, this is what has arrived." That is all. And then place your energy into a commitment: "Through a growing consciousness, I will create something better. I will repair and remove this creation, through what I do today towards tomorrow." The more your energy is placed in this light, what is created of yesterday dissolves and carries no farther.

Forgiveness, then, is in the action of committing to consciousness. Not in great crying regret and pleading for forgiveness from God or others, which goes nowhere. Rather, be compassionate to what was created yesterday and committed to what will be created tomorrow. Understand clearly the laws of karma, of cause and effect, and realize that you are the small creator of your reality and existence. You will not know what happened yesterday in its entirety, for yesterday is a very long and extensive story that moves beyond your birth into many lives. At present, you do not remember or see that thread of your being moving through the lives. Yet, you *can* see what has arrived in your moment, now. All that you are is a product of all that you have created in all of your lives. Your energy is meant to be placed into what comes, into what is being shaped *now*.

Now listen to this: if the potter were to be overcome with regret and shame over all the broken pots, he would not be able to focus and place his full attention on the pot in his hands. The pot in his hands requires absolute attention so that no air pockets and no stones are included. Listen to the teaching of the potter and give your full attention to what is at present before you. All the broken pots in your trail, behind you, are there. They have given you knowledge and skill. You may not remember most of them, but the impact of their breaking and failure are there. What you hold in your pain are those stories. Listen to them. They are the knowledge of how those pots broke, of what broke.

Your vital energy must be given to the pot in your hands now. You can say, "The neck of that one was too narrow, not generous enough, did not receive enough. Therefore this one must be wider." Or, "The walls of that one were far too thin and sensitive and fragile. Therefore the walls of this must be thicker." Or one could say, "This one was built in too much of a hurry, with too much impatience, without thought, and therefore had no use." All the lessons in your pain can be there as you shape this present pot, so that what you create now includes your knowledge and what you have learned.

Realize with patience that the pot you are shaping now will also have imperfections, unconsciousness, and that you won't learn about those until it goes through its firing. So we are asking you to rejoice in the process of your evolution. Be patient and compassionate with it.

Every pot, both intact and broken, is sacred. That is a powerful statement to hold in your being. In the grace of supreme consciousness, there is no judgment. There is only a compassionate beckoning forward. If you were to cry and lament, "I cannot create an intact pot! I am no good as a potter! I shouldn't exist!" the compassionate one of grace would say, "Try again. You are made of beauty. You are made of the finest clay. Find it. You are an artist as are all beings and you have the same capacity as all beings. Try again. Find it."

There is only the beckoning forward, and the punishment that you experience is not from God, is not from grace and the great source of light and presence. The punishment you experience is simply the laws of karma. Do you purposely include fractures? Do you purposely include dysfunction in what you are shaping? Then you will exist in dysfunction and your life, your creation, will not work for you. If you innocently include fractures and dysfunction, your life also will show you and your innocence will lift into awareness. If you purposely include fractures and dysfunction, then you will purposely create pain.

There is a great difference between these two: one who acts in knowledge of rightness and chooses it not, and one who acts in innocence of rightness. The one who chooses consciously to act in dysfunction, to include it in their life and what they create, has stepped into a realm of power whereby they invite powerful lessons into themselves, experiences like hammers and great fires that shape them. The firing then is greater and the kiln burns hotter, until the fracture seams are understood and the dysfunction is finished. Therefore grace only beckons all beings forward.

Punishment is self-inflicted. It is an inherent law of matter that evolves all beings in all forms forward. It is not, then, truly punishment but simply cause and effect. If you place your hand in a fire for too long and do not listen to the signals that you are being injured, then the injury will be very great indeed - cause and effect.

We ask you to consider patience, to not be in a hurry nor impatient with your being. You exist right now, in one lifetime, one bead on a string of many beads. It avails you to be patient. Being impatient is a sign of unconsciousness, of child-like unawareness. Patience comes from knowing the greatness of the process, the beauty of the pot. To build a truly perfect pot requires the time to find the most wonderful clay, to prepare it perfectly with patience, to develop the skill and awareness through many lives and experiences, and to take the time needed to shape the pot with great foresight and hindsight. Patience builds consciousness. When the potter can be compassionate towards himself or herself, and patient with what has come before, then he or she is not pushed and hurried and unfocused.

Reflect on your limitations and pain, your family web of pain, what you realize and don't realize, and to the centre of this breathe patience. Breathe compassion. Let the story unfold as it will. Let the pain emerge, and come and go as it will. Learn how to listen to the pain without being afraid of it, without going into a reaction of regret, guilt, or anger. Do not get caught up in trying to suppress or do anything with it. Just let it come. Observe the broken pot - where it broke, how it broke and why it broke - and then walk away, carrying that knowledge into what you create now. Be patient as you stare at the pot that broke until you can realize where, how, and why it broke. This is as vital as what you create anew. Let there be the time and patience given to be aware of what has occurred and what has led to now. Recapitulate, reflect, and allow the past to reveal itself. Allow the illusions and constructed belief systems to stand in the light.

The temple fire looks at the hands of all who approach it and asks, "What has the walking friend brought as a gift for the sitting friend?"

The sitting friend is the inner fire, and the walking friend is the body that goes forth in the outer world. All actions of the body are to be dedicated to the Inner Friend.

*Litany of Fire
Atarch-Niyaesh*

*I*mpatience, then, is to be avoided and counselled against. If you see the beauty within and understand all that has been said here and all that you hear of who you are, that does not mean that you can become it in the next instant. There is a sacred and powerful process towards truth that you must be patient with. You must realize every step of your own journey. Silent emerging of freedom comes in this way - a full encompassing of the past, present and future, as though they were one; being able to look at the broken pots of those around you in the same light of compassion and non-judgment as you look at your own, in fact calling them your own. Learn from everything and everyone. In the spirit of patience, you *will* learn. In the spirit of judgment, regret and guilt, you will not learn.

Karma, then, is not to be feared as a judgmental law coming from God, destiny, or fate. Karma is to be understood as the potter's process of shaping the most beautiful pot, which can hold supreme consciousness, the sweetest water, and keep it fresh and alive, to be poured out to others. Do not become caught in any other belief that anything is not in your hands. It *is* in your hands.

If the potter were to hold his hands up and say, "These are not in my hands", nothing would be created except by others. Do you do that? Do you take the clay into your own hands and claim the creation that you are existing within as your own? Or do you hold your hands in the air and say, "I didn't create this. I cannot." Then you are allowing your being to be impacted by others and taking no responsibility for consciousness or unconsciousness. You are in the illusion of victim-hood, feeling the victim of karma, of life and of others. This is the most contracted and unconscious state of the human being. This is the beaten dog in the corner with no loving owner, facing death, like the dogs of Egypt. That is their agreement. They have agreed to victim-hood. Do you agree to it? Do you agree to unconsciousness, that you can shape nothing and have shaped nothing? If you agree to that, then close the book.

 This is a teaching towards consciousness, towards nurturing and building truth of who you are. You are beauty. You are God. You are the artist of divine principles. You are not separate. You are not poor and ignorant. Sathya Sai Baba says, "I am God and you are God. The difference between us is that I know this and you do not." What a great difference that is. So much we cannot fathom is held in those words. What does it mean to know that "I am God"? It means to be beyond the laws of unconsciousness, matter and form, to be in the essence of supreme light and consciousness.

 As the teachers all point, they say, "Come through the doorway. Leave victim-hood and unconsciousness behind. Know who you are. There is no karma beyond the doorway. There is simply a greater and greater flowering of beauty and harmony." What is placed into the beginning will determine the ending. The dawn of a thought, relationship, birth and event determines its fruit and outcome. Absolute consciousness brings into the beginning of everything what is required at the ending. Therefore there is no suffering, no surprises, no shattering events as it is discovered that what was placed at the beginning was wrong. Rightness is understood and placed into the start of things, deepening, expanding and growing towards the ending. This is the use of karma in its highest form.

Create tomorrow today by realizing yesterday and understanding this powerful dynamic of this linear realm of cause and effect. To study the physics and chemistry of matter is to understand the physics and the chemistry of unconsciousness, beingness and consciousness. It is holographic, and you are immersed in this realm of matter, of chemistry, physics, mathematics - this and this results in that. We are positioned here because this is the most exact placement for evolving supreme consciousness. Just as in the pure mathematical understanding, there are no illusions: this plus this equals that. And that is all there is to it. Every time you add vinegar to soda you receive the same reaction. This is the same law you face. This is karma. What you put in, you receive. What you add to determines what you end up with. In every aspect of this realm, there is this law. If you add into your equations the finest and the highest intentions and materials, you lift into another octave of results.

We leave this now, this discourse on the laws of karma.

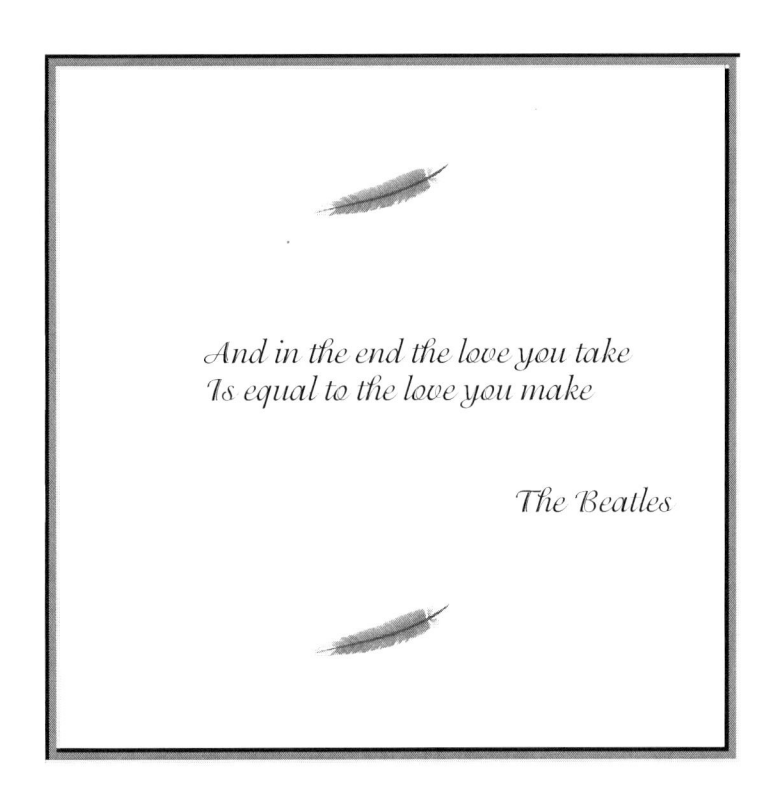

*And in the end the love you take
Is equal to the love you make*

The Beatles

Do not lay up for yourselves treasure on earth, where moth and rust consume and where thieves break in and steal, but lay up for yourselves treasures in heaven, where neither moth nor rust consumes and where thieves do not break in and steal. For where your treasure is, there will your heart be also.

Matthew 6.19

Patience & Understanding With The Process

$\mathcal{U}$nderstanding leads to patience. To understand where you are in your process of healing and realization can gain you patience and understanding of what has come before and what lies ahead. The stages of healing are the same as the stages of a lifetime. They can be charted along the same pattern of child, adolescent, young adult, full adult, elder, and wisdom being. Stages of development occur also in healing and realization, which are woven, for it is the lack of healing, the unconsciousness in body and soul, which limits realization and awareness. As the being heals in all ways, so does realization grow.

From the very first infant stage, there is raw awareness of emotions, of pain, with no possibility to cope, comprehend, or do anything, a naked experience of what is felt and experienced. It is a most tender time of being shaped by experiences, pain, and emotions, building the foundation and fabric of self, of the sense of *I AM* within the context of this life and beyond. What is being put in can seldom be pushed away or incorporated beyond just reception.

Depending on the degree of trauma and difficulty, there is sometimes a forced need to cope, to move into reaction. But usually, all experience is lived "as-is" and stored deep in the core to be made sense of later. In many it is never comprehended. It is put into a silence where there is no consciousness, stored so deeply in the core experience that it swiftly becomes unconscious. It impregnates the very nature of the being who operates unconsciously from there for the rest of their life and lives. The infant and the child have no ability to do anything else. They have no ability to stop the experience, make sense of it, or forgive it.

This, then, is the first primal stage, and if you look into yourself and others, you can still see it - unconsciously held experience causing response, reaction, fears, temperament and ways of being, though the person has no understanding of why. They are just this way, reacting, responding senselessly to the experiences of life, without being rational, without there being any clear reason. That being, whether they are a child or an adult, is in the stage of their healing and realization that is unconsciousness, which is the first room.

It is the room that must be walked forth from into the second stage of healing and realization, which can be loosely called the adolescent, the growing child. This is where the awareness of feeling and irrational behaviour has become sharp, the senseless emotion and responses are being noticed. The consciousness is beginning to look at itself, to need to understand. This is a watching time, of light beginning to enter in to reveal states of being that are detrimental, causing sometimes illness, sometimes great disruption in the life. Yet this is still a very young and difficult time when the being is often trying to submerge this awareness back down into an unconscious place, dismiss it and carry on. Yet they can't because life continues to be disrupted by what is felt and the conclusions, reactions and responses that arise.

This stage is the beginning of awareness of what creates the feeling, causes the fear, hatred or anger to arise. It is a time of noticing, "Whenever this happens, I feel that way. Whenever this condition surrounds me, I become like that."

Also at this time a desire for change arises, a need for it to be different, to be free. So this childlike time is the time of what we will call projection. "This person is doing this to me. This behaviour causes this feeling within me and this situation in the world or in this room causes me to be like that and throws me into this place. Therefore, if that person or these conditions would change, I'd improve, I'd be better."

This is a necessary stage of realizing. It is a time when the outside world is holding a mirror of experiences the individual needs to understand and see. However, the individual at this stage only sees it one way, that the outside is causing the inside. And yet this time must be. This is a stage of realizing what triggers one's being into closure, depression, and anger, noticing more and more who, where and what. It is a time where one remembers relationships that resemble the present ones, that caused the same feelings. Often one starts to see through what others do to cause pain, what is wrong. This is a great, difficult time and as you look around you, you will see many who are there. They live in defensiveness.

The adolescent stage of awakening to what causes one to feel the way they're feeling - this is where the human being is largely entangled and at war. This is the stage that is in the courthouses, where one is striving to establish blame and have it rectified from the outside. But one's inner experience is on the inside. Look around you and see this stage. See the entanglement, the attempt to establish who, where and how, and if *that* can be solved, if it can be clearly proven who is doing it and what it has done to me, then I will have peace and resolution. I can be free of this experience. And the other person has had to pay, to admit, "Yes, it was me who was doing that and caused you this." Then that person must change and never do it again.

This is living outside of oneself in the projection. It is a necessary stage of realizing what one carries inside. As the emotions and experiences begin to surface, one needs to do something with them. One needs to realize where they came from and what conditions caused them. They need to identify the individuals and kind of human nature that creates pain, suffering, and wrongness.

In this stage, one is not realizing their part. They are only realizing what else caused it, who did it. It is a time of trying to establish blame and perceive one's existence through the effects others have caused. As we said, much of the world and humanity is in this adolescent stage of healing and realization. It is a time of victim-hood, and to live outside of oneself is to live very vulnerably, outside of one's centre of power in one's self. It is to have no control, no direction and no true ability to create change. It is to live vulnerable and empty.

As the adolescent moves into the young adult phase, there begins to be the repetition of experiences. The same experiences of childhood, school and relationship keep repeating. The young adult awareness, then, begins enter into the self and question, "Was this always just caused on the outside or did I have a part in it?" The uncanny repetition of relationships and experiences begins to inform the young adult that perhaps there is more to it. Seeing that the same treatment is received from the husband as from the father, the same experience repeating itself, leaving one partner for another, the young adult begins to ask these questions. It is the beginning of understanding better what is in the mirror of the world around, and what one's part could be in changing one's experience.

This is the phase of healing and realization where often one begins to reach for a different kind of help than the court system and blame system.   One asks, "What can I do? Not only what should *you* do, but what can *I* do?" This is the beginning of a turning point in the individual's maturing, where they start to realize that they do play a part. They can chart and notice the patterns, conditions, relationships and situations that cause the same feelings and responses to arise every time. And in this, they begin to feel the sense of choice.

As the young adult moves into the full adult, they begin to realize this choice that is always there: to choose situations, relationships, and responses rather than just succumb or be driven by emotion, reaction, and unconscious response. The adult phase, then, is where one is beginning to truly live inside oneself rather than outside. One learns skills for changing responses, finding subtler inner choices of how to react to situations and what kind of situations and relationships to choose to be in.

The adult is in a stage of choice and this is the time when healing can become swift. Realization begins to really enter, that there *was* choice, even before now. One learns to make choices that change one's life, choosing different ways of existing in the emotional being, of responding to life, and perhaps even beginning to help others to learn the same. This is the maturity of an adult. This, then, is where one can begin to let go of the past in its raw, dynamic impact, to actually move away from all the pain and anguish held in one's being. One re-learns how to respond and how to choose which situations to be in, learning what to do with people that have caused pain, and what kind of people cause this pain. One either creates separation from the offending persons, or creates a loving, compassionate response, learning how to be with those individuals so that more pain and anguish is not developed.

When this adult phase is completed, one enters into the elder. The perspective of an elder is distinctly different and much greater. Remember these stages do not correspond to the age an individual may be in. They are just the stages in purity. One might enter into the elder phase midway through life. One may have the adult phase at the end of a life and never reach the elder stage. These stages of consciousness are not defined by age, though they often correspond to it. The elder, then, begins to understand their being, their experiences in life and beyond life. They begin to perceive that this life is only one of many and that the conditions of this life were chosen for a purpose. They were chosen out of the great theme and purpose of evolution of that being.

The elder, then, begins to expand completely beyond blame, projection and entanglement in the conditions of one life, and they are able to place their experiences into a greater purpose, seeing that the conditions of birth, childhood, country and lifetime all fit into the purpose of their evolving soul. The elder begins to seek the greater picture of their soul through the lives, seeing how the distinct nature and challenges of a lifetime fit into the ongoing progression and theme. The elder is free of that life because the elder encompasses more than that life.

To seek understanding of the elder in any of the earlier phases can be ineffectual, because each stage is necessary and must complete itself before the next one can truly be entered. Therefore, if the other stages are not complete, understanding of one's past lives and birth conditions would be information just sitting in the mind as empty knowledge. If the adult phase of how to choose different situations and responses is not there, the information of the greater theme is really of little avail. One who is in the adolescent stage needs to understand what the feelings are that are emerging fast and furious, what the wrongness is in that person yelling. They must be right there. They must see who is causing what and why.

Appreciate and have patience with the phase that you are in and that you see others in. The elder, then, beginning to see the great scope of lives and purpose, can finally let go and not feel victim in any way whatsoever, but rather see choice and purpose. The elder, in so seeing, chooses differently in all interactions, in all lives to come. The elder leads into the wisdom being, who is truly free and has access to universal and divine wisdom. This stage within the lifetime corresponds symbolically to death and mergence.

See, then, these stages: raw reception of experience, with no capacity to incorporate or understand; then the beginning of capacity, moving from subconscious suppression into raw feeling, needing to establish where the feeling comes from, what and who causes it, the importance of the court system stage to establish wrong and right and what cannot be lived with; the stage where one internalizes more and realizes the patterns that repeat and that one actually had a part in it, that by that reaction and choice it continued to happen; the maturity entering in, moving away from projection into living within responsibility and choice and seeing one's place and part; that phase then moving into greater wisdom, a final ability to see what one did choose and why and how it was all one's choice, essentially, all along, that there never really was a victim, but only a need to experience life in that way for this reason; then the true healing, realization and entering into wisdom.

The Doctrine Of Oneness

What is the identity, reality and experience of oneness? What is the self in light of the identity of oneness and what is the relationship of self to this oneness?

The most essential truth is this great, vast beingness that we are all a part of. Every being, every aspect of creation is all part of this great presence of oneness. In the most essential nature and truth, there is this identity of oneness, one great being. All is one great entity, one great creation, all woven, all part of. Not chaotic, confused and separate, but all one. All beings and aspects of creation, every stone, plant, and star at their very core are one. Every creature within the sea is part of the sea; the sea is part of the air that rises from it, as are clouds that land their moisture on the mountains, all creatures, all humans upon the earth, all elements throughout the universe, all stars, atoms and atomic matter, all light, all suns and non-physical light and all the consciousness that is part of all forms within the entire universe – all is one, and it is all evolving together. It is one great presence, one great beingness, one great godliness.

This is the doctrine of oneness: that there is, in essential truth, no individual, no self that sits in separation. To identify one's being as a separate self and stop there is wrong. The doctrine of oneness is saying, "You are all, and that person over there is you. You are part of all beings and all beings are a part of you." This identity, then, is to address all beings as though they were you, to identify that closely with all beings, all nature and all creation as though it were a part of you.

We bring forth the golden rule: *Do unto others as you would have them do unto you.* Listen to that ancient statement for it is a rule indeed. It is a key to living in the identity of the oneness, to address all your existence as though it were you.

How does one do this, then, but through the heart? The heart knows rightness. It knows what it needs. You know what it feels to be loved or not loved, respected, honoured, hated, disregarded, or listened to. Your heart knows and is the same heart as all beings carry. So through your heart, you know this oneness and you know what all beings need. To treat another the way that you wish to be treated is to exist within this reality of oneness and to give unto all beings as though they were all you and you were all they. The heart is the place of knowing this truth.

There are some, then, whose hearts are so impacted with pain and hatred that they cannot hear what love, respect, or honour are. But deep within them, in the pure beginning of that very heart, is that same nature. That being is just a being in great need of healing and process and requires great patience, and the truth is that their very essential heart is the same as yours and the very essential way for them to heal is through love, compassion, and patience. Love your enemy. It is easy to love those who love you. That is not what I'm asking.

I'm asking you to love your enemy, for your enemy is the one who truly needs love. Where does that come from, that teaching? It comes from understanding the doctrine of oneness, that through reaching to that other being with what their heart really needs, they will heal. Through giving back to them hatred and anger, you'll only increase their isolation and their separateness, their violence, their wrongness. And through reaching through that, to that heart that is the same as your own, you will begin to stir and awaken their healing, for what they really need is to be respected and loved and heard and if you were to hear into their story, perhaps you would understand why they had gotten so far away from their heart of truth. Their whole story would no doubt bring compassion and understanding to you and help you to give them what they really need. Not what they apparently may deserve, but what they actually really need.

    The experience of oneness, then, is to experience all beings, all creation, as one body, as one family. Community is a family. The earth is your body, the creatures and everything around you is all part of you and that is the experience of oneness. The bird singing is not singing outside of you but is singing within you, and the river's sparkling light is not sparkling outside of you but within you. The river is your blood. The air is your breath. And everything about you is part of you. And even the beggar and even the urchin and even the being that you despise are part of you.

    The experience of oneness would say then, that person over there who is angry, who is yelling - have you ever felt that way?

Have you ever felt that anger, have you ever given vent to that anger? Have you ever been like that? Because that is you as well. You are there as well. And perhaps you weren't as angry or as loud, but did you feel as angry or as loud? Can you identify with everything you see around you and realize that you are all one? Through identifying, even with the negativity, and saying "That, too, is a part of my being." And listening, "What does that part of my being need? What does my being need?" Listen to the heart. What is that being really saying? They're saying "I am despairing, I am despised, I don't believe in my life. I am isolated, I am scared." Anger can say all that. Have you ever felt that way? What does that being need? Do you remember what you needed? It is all one.

The experience of oneness, then, is to give unto others exactly what your heart knows it needed. And as you give unto them, you give unto yourself. As you give love to another, you are loving yourself. And as you have compassion for others, you have compassion for yourself. It is indivisible, all beings around you and your being. And truly as you address life all around you, you are addressing your own being. This, then, is the experience of oneness.

The Place Of Self In Oneness

The self arises from a lifetime. The body, emotions, character, and life conditions give rise to the egoic self, which has great purpose and place. It is not to be negated, disregarded, or struggled against and told, "You cannot be here." Self, or egoic nature, is not wrong in essence. It is a part of this picture.

The self is like a doorway. Through the doorway is the great, outer, vast world of creation; inside the doorway is the same - a great, inner vastness of presence, experience, and beingness. The self is a distinct, unique doorway that receives the world and communicates to the world. The self is a creator who creates ways and navigates through the world, communicating and directing the experience within the world. Where one gets lost is when one thinks there is only that self, that that self is the great creator and that there is nothing else. The egoic self needs to be in a very clear and open relationship to soul, or greater Self, and to the vastness of Presence, the true being within, the oneness.

The self needs to learn what it is a creator *for*. It is an experiencer and a communicator for the soul. It is a scout, taking the being into new territory, perceiving, receiving, cataloguing, experiencing, and creating response. And yet every step of this ought to be guided by linking into the wisdom, into the oneness that is available and is a part of all beings. Allow the self to settle into a deep place, to dissolve for a moment and listen into the heart, perhaps into the wisdom teachers throughout time, and more than that, into the wisdom that is within all beings. How to respond? How to go forward? What is the meaning of this day, of this experience? Tap in always to greater Self and bring that forth to the doorway of egoic self. Then begin to shape and create one's character and life around a truth that is brought from within.

Self then is to get the materials for its creation from beyond the self, from the greater beingness and the wisdom within, placing that into the uniqueness of the character and the shaping of a life. Have a daily practice of meditation or some manner of moving within to receive the wisdom, to feel into the truth, to know into the heart, and then to come back into the surficial distinctness of self, into the will, the creator, the mind. Bring that forth and speak it, act it, live it, and shape it into one's work, relationships, and building of a life. This will make the path between the doorway and the deep within easy to find, well trod and travelled, so the flow of heart, understanding, and wisdom can come easily into mind, tongue, action, and character.

Understand, then, the relationship of self to oneness and to soul. Self is a necessary part of a lifetime and of an evolving being. It is a place where one learns to bring the true nature of divine presence into manifestation, relationship, parenting, and creating a world.

Consider a world shaped by the doctrine of oneness, by individuals operating from a place of oneness flowing into their individuality, from an understanding that there is only one great existence in a myriad thousand million forms of expression, that there is only one great purpose that sits as latent potential and wisdom within the heart of all beings, within the very atomic nature of all matter, and that it needs to be accessed, understood and brought forth into the creative principals of mind, will, self and character so that a world is shaped around it. Think of a world based on this, of a system of government, community and family that is at ease with this. You can see examples of this already. You can see beings living in commitment and relationship to God, truth, and love. This is good.

Yet you can also see where it falls short, where some think *they* have the truth and others don't. Whenever an entity, church or country feels that it has the only way, it is falling short of the doctrine of oneness and is creating separation. Though they may have in place an accessing of wisdom, truth and love within, it is still cramped and limited to a version or dogma, a protection and separation.

So you do not see, on any scale, this comprehension of oneness in place in the world. If you were to see it, there would be a true unity amongst countries, religions and churches. There would be respect, compassion, and an understanding that the heart of all beings - animal, human, plant - is one. The elements and atomic matter that sit as substrate for all creation are within all forms, and the light of the sun falls equally upon all forms. You are like a flower in your distinctness, fragrance, and colour, in your medicine and qualities. And yet the sun that shines upon you is what opened the seed and called you forth and nurtured you. It is the same sun that called forth the flower beside you. The sun is like the great presence of unity and oneness, and the flowers and all the plants are like the individual characters that express life and truth. In the world of plants there is no separation. It is all the same principle of sun calling forth seed, of moisture moved by sun. The great light of the sun is God, and all the individual forms are the selves and characters developing in its light.

Watch how the plant that has the best exposure to sunlight and moisture develops into the most beautiful, full form of itself. Place yourself that way, in full exposure to wisdom and oneness, to the great light of consciousness, and allow your being to fully flower and develop into the truth that it is. Realize that the physical sun too is just a physical fire, and that the light of consciousness that is behind the creation of all suns, planets, matter and beings is the light of God, the divine light. It emanates through all creation, through *you*, taking you into your uniqueness, your evolving of lives, your shape.

You aren't in isolation. Learn the well-trodden path of self to soul to atma, or Great Presence. Understand the doctrine of oneness to allow your identity and reality to follow. And teach it; teach it to your children. Bring it to your interactions with life. In this doctrine of oneness you can see how self, as real as it is when you are sitting within it, is really a temporary illusion, just a brief foothold, and that the true nature of your conscious existence is not labelled self at all - the doctrine of 'no self', then.

You will hear it being taught that self is illusion, is passing, fleeting, is *Maya*. You will hear it being taught that all matter, all created forms, are Maya and illusion. Understand it in that way. They are distinctly present. They are real. And yet in essence they are just the light of truth. They are just the great presence of divine entity, the shadows of Supreme Beingness, reflections of God.

And so, *your self is a form and structure that evolves you*. As long as you are caught in isolation, that's all there is, and have no consciousness that you are part of the great being, you are caught in an illusion. You are trapped in an unconsciousness, and you are trapped in an experience that is small.

Do Not Judge

Teachers of humanity have taught to treat everyone as though they were God, as though each were an angel, or your own child or own master. This is the way. Never treat another as less than yourself, as less than God, for that diminishes your self. This great teaching, this great expanding of perception, will change the world. It will change the way you understand your life, the way you see others around you, and the way you relate to all your experiences. The more you hammer into form a separation, blame, projection, and treating of others with judgment, the more you lock yourself into a cage, into unconsciousness and suffering. Never, then, see others in judgment. It has been taught – *do not judge*. The only one who could possibly judge is one who is omniscient, all-knowing, and that one never would judge. So really there isn't such thing as judgment and there can't be.

The only way you could rightly judge another being is with a full repertoire of knowledge as to who that being is. And yet then you would know that that being is just the same as you. Therefore to judge that being is to judge yourself, which leads to self-condemnation. *Do not judge* – three words, a great principle of the doctrine of oneness. This is the golden rule.

Essentially, it's all so simple and the more you move into an experience of truth within your being, the simpler life becomes.

It is only complex when caught in forms, emotion, mind, separateness and the battles that occur in that way. How to live, how to create peace and experience abundance and harmony is essentially profoundly simple. The experience of oneness is that of simplicity and abundance. As you treat others rightfully, lovingly, and compassionately, so then do others treat you and your experience becomes more beautiful. Others seek and befriend you, giving unto you. The human being desires so much to break its isolation and separateness, and so by treating them as yourself and your brethren, they respond and give in return. So the experience of oneness is of growing abundance, simplicity, and joy.

As you enjoin with all beings and celebrate their unique selves in light of the oneness, the world becomes a beautiful, flowering place. You perceive those that could be difficult and negative in a different way than someone else because you have given unto them. You are choosing to experience them from a place of oneness and love.

The experience of separation is the opposite. If a being were to be addressed from a place of distrust and separation, you would receive their distrust and negativity.

Which Bell Do You Wish to Ring?

All individuals are capable of many responses. Which bell do you wish to ring? Which reality do you wish to nurture and live in? You will understand your reality swiftly, for love has great rewards, and it helps you trust what truth is. As you step out and treat the other as though they were you, your experience of truth grows greater and you trust. And as your trust grows greater you learn that it is safe to go within, to go beyond the character of self into the vastness of breath and light. You learn to hear and trust the voice of wisdom that guides you through all the lives, for you see it brings only bounty, fruitfulness, and an expanding sense of place and embrace.

An individual being is like an orchestra, capable of harmonious music or great discordant sound. What do you call forth? What you have called forth surrounds you in sound and experience. Which bell do you wish to ring?

All of you are undertaking some sort of Sadhana. What exactly is the real meaning of Sadhana? Give up body attachment and try to experience atmic bliss. How do you attain that bliss? It can be attained only through Prema (love). If you have pure love, all your suffering will be removed. Therefore, cultivate pure and selfless love.

Supposing, you come across a person on the road who is inimical to you. If you hate him and move away from him considering him as your enemy, the hatred between you and him increases further. On the other hand, if you greet him lovingly saying "Hello! How are you?" naturally he would respond also with love. Thus, when you both greet each other lovingly, there will be no scope for hatred persisting anymore. As is your feeling towards others, so is their feeling.

The same idea is contained in the Vedic declaration: Yad Bhavam Tad Bhavati (as is the feeling, so is the result). Sometimes, we may have negative feelings against others.

But these negative feelings should be considered just like passing clouds. They come and go. The sun may not be visible when it is covered by thick clouds. The moment the clouds move away, the sun is visible.

Similarly, when your negative feelings scatter away, what remains is pure love. You can achieve anything in this world with love. In fact, you can have the entire world under your control through love. People say they are meditating both in the morning and evening. But, what kind of meditation is this? What benefit are they deriving out of it? How long does its effect last? Not even for a moment. Remember, all worldly matters are like passing clouds. Therefore, do not involve yourself too much in them.

Bhagavan Sathya Sai Baba
Sanathan Sarati
March 2004

Understanding The World

*A*gain, to understand this world, have patience to its process. How do you perceive the world? Do you listen to the news? Do you read the papers and hear what others say? You cannot help but do that. How are others understanding the world? What are the commonly held conclusions and beliefs upon hearing the news and listening to each other?

We are teaching you to have a different perspective to view the world from. You must hear what is occurring in the world, but you also must have a different perspective in order not to despair, or become fearful and discouraged. You could lose your place of equanimity and understanding of the great oneness of all creation. If you were to look at one picture of a person frowning or crying, would you then say that that person was a negative person? When you hear the story on the news, would you then say that humanity is like that? Would you draw conclusions based on that photograph or that newscast about that country or those people? Would you draw conclusions as to what those people were like in that religion and country based on what you had heard?

We are telling you your perspective is too small. We are telling you that by listening to it, you are entering into conclusions and experiences based on too small a perspective. If you were to look at the life of an individual who was extremely poor and begged and had very little, would you say that that soul is impoverished? Or if you were to look at the life of an individual who was born crippled and incapable and remained so their entire life, would you say that that being was crippled and incapable?

    We are telling you your perspective is too small. Do you understand that your perspective, when based on a photo, a news story, or a lifetime, is too small? It endangers you to go into despair, into judgment and into a complete lack of understanding of what is really occurring. You are highly endangered by listening to and observing the world from this small perspective. Going back to the photograph of the frown, you need a whole album of photos of that individual; you need to see them through all the stages of their life. Perhaps that day the frown was one of great compassion for something that had happened. You need to know the story that led into and out of that photograph. You need the greater picture of that individual before you can base your feelings and your sense of reality.

    It is the same, then, for the soul within a lifetime. If you only see that lifetime, do you understand that being? Do you know why they were born crippled? Do you know what purposes were being worked-out within that being, what karma was beautifully served? Do you know the story that led into and out of that life? So you see your perspective needs to be bigger to truly grasp what you are seeing and to understand the world. Do you understand that country's history, psychology, and spirituality? Do you understand the karma of that country, the story that led into and out of that newscast? You will not know such stories. You will not have such great perspective, but you must assume it. You must sit in a place that realizes the vastness of these stories, the great purposes that are being worked out in humanity and the world and you must move into a place of compassion and realization – that there is great purpose in tragedy, and great direction in the human soul. It is relentless, and always leading to more realization.

The stages of healing we spoke earlier of apply here as well. They apply globally to humanity moving from adolescence into adulthood. The great stages of development are at play. We cannot freeze one stage and judge that humanity is foul and should not exist and is wrong based on one court battle, war, photo, or century. Your perspective must widen for you to not fall into despair and judgment.

Now you would say, "How can I not despair when I hear of such things as a whole gymnasium of parents and children being killed?" And we say, you *are* to grieve. You *are* to know the wrongness for the great affront to their beings, for the tragedy. But then you are *not* to sink into despair. You are not to draw the great conclusion that leads to depression and loss of hope, for you do not know the story within those individuals and what their death served. You do not know the greater picture that you only witness the carnal and physical event of. You do not know the great purposes that were being moved through in the holocaust and or the outcome for all the millions of souls that sprung from there. The soul does not die, and the individual beingness, the consciousness of soul and spirit, does not die. Only the physical shell, that was crushed or shot, sickened and died.

From the greatest destruction and crumbling and despair, the soul will spring into the opposite, into grasping and claiming life and seeking beauty, harmony, purpose and reason. Out of every despicable, sordid, and painful event, the soul continues to spring forth and reach evermore for what is right and true and eternal. You must have this great perspective: death is temporary; death is passage. The eternal nature of life, soul, and presence survives these things, moves onward and makes use of it.

There is purpose found in everything, just as in the healing of your own life, discovering the purpose of choosing those traumatic situations of childhood. As the human being becomes the wisdom being, they also realize the purposes in their own history, and as that is reached there is no more choosing of such crude, traumatic ways of existing. You must have a greater perspective for understanding the world, beyond now, beyond self, emotion, and judgment.

Whenever you hear the most terrible thing, let it coalesce into a photograph, saying, "This is a sad, terrible photograph, but I don't know the picture leading in or leading out. And so I will hold that photograph in prayer and I will hold it up into the great light of eternal presence, knowing that all that springs forth from this pain and tragedy will lead further into the light for each soul that dies there. Each individual that suffered will reach away from suffering. Each one who died brutally will reach for life that is free of brutality. For each negativity, there is the opposite. There is a light-filled, essential optimism that must enter in, and it will as you move beyond emotion, judgment, mind, and self into the oneness and sense of divine truth that you all are. As you look at the entire entity evolving throughout creation, you will see that it is all slowly evolving into more and more beauty and consciousness, and that it is best not to get caught behind a boulder and see the world encaged from a small place.

Dharmic Understanding & Action

We show a picture of a wheel rolling, slowly, methodically, with all its spokes, a wheel with a direction and a purpose. Dharma is that wheel rolling within this temporal world. It is the wheel of a lifetime, the legs carrying you forward. It is each creation within your life, each action, year, phase, and indeed, each life building upon each other. The dharmic wheel spins forward, moving one into greater and greater consciousness, rolling down through the deep, dark valley of pain, unconsciousness, and anguish, getting mired in mud and yet always striving to move and always moving, even imperceptibly. It moves on through the mire, carrying the mud upon itself until it all falls away. The wheel moves in and out of the light, in and out of days and eras, the wheel of existence manifest. To define dharma is to open the consciousness to the great wheel of right-existence, the right-purpose and right-direction of existence.

Life is to be understood as the wheel of one's manifestations, of one's existence, and the process of God, consciousness, and all beings evolving. Dharma is right-action, directed movement, forward motion, and conscious development of life through existence. Dharma must be understood in expansive terms, in less expansive terms, and in very practical terms.

One can look at the great wheel of life purpose that sits within civilizations and humanity evolving throughout time. One can get the picture of the developments of consciousness through those great wheels turning. One can look at the wheel of one's own life that has been incurred and created, the direction that one's life has gone, what one has manifested is continuing to manifest.

One can look at dharma in terms of the progression of lives of an individual and how the wheel keeps turning, resuming where it left off, what it gathers in its course. How straight and true does the wheel turn? How likely is it to be mired in mud or to lead into dark vales of unconsciousness? The dharmic wheel is the embodiment of the consciousness in that being. It is all built into that wheel, its shape, its ability to go true and straight, to move easily or not. How does the wheel turn? How consciously does it turn? How conscious are you from one life to the next? How conscious are you from one decade to the next or from one day to the next? How able are you to see actions and results, see what sits at the basis of creation's events? How clearly can you see the outcomes that have come from the outset? How clearly can you see the wheel turning in your life?

Dharma then, in a closer meaning, is this attention given to consciousness, to truth, to purifying one's actions, beliefs, and thoughts, to constantly reshaping one's relationship to life and others according to the higher values of the doctrine of oneness - the values of love, of living in truth or in the light. This is a closer meaning of the word dharma. It is spiritualized, light-filled action and engaged consciousness that is choosing to exist in these ways of building more and more beauty and rightness. Dharma – right action, right speech, right thought. Watch the thread of that moving from the outside towards the inside, the rightness that occurs in what you do, say and create. It comes from the rightness of how you believe and what you think, what you generate within your heart and mind. This, then, is dharma.

Living in dharma, in dharmic thought, in right thought, in dharmic speech – what does this mean? Speech begins to create outwardly. It manifests what one thinks and believes and it begins to create a structure outwardly in the world. It may be a structure of feelings or belief systems, and it may go so far as to be a structure of what is set in motion within the world. Right speech, then, is speech that has the attention within it, is not careless, and knows what it will create. Right action, or what one actually does to manifest right thought, then follows, a stream of true beingness coming from the thought layer to the action level. This is dharma - existing in a thoroughness of purity and intention that manifests the highest values and the truest truths that one is capable of understanding and living with.

Better than a speech of a thousand vain words is one thoughtful word, which brings peace to the mind. Better than a poem of a thousand vain verses is one thoughtful line, which brings peace to the mind. Better than a hundred poems of vain stanzas is one word of the dharma that brings peace to the mind.

One who conquers himself is greater than another who conquers a thousand times a thousand men on the battlefield. Be victorious over yourself and not over others. When you attain victory over yourself, not even the gods can turn it into defeat.

The Dhammapada

*U*nderstand, then, this simple, ancient word, for it acts like a key that can open a doorway to orienting one's actions, the meaning of one's days, and the choices one makes. Is it dharmic? Is this work dharmic that I'm considering? Does this job placement or this line of study in university have dharmic content? See how the use of a word that is deeply pregnant with meaning can be a key or a guide, examining then what one thinks and does with that question – is it dharmic? Does it direct the wheel straight and true? Will it strengthen the turning of my wheel to carry me into freedom and light, into a true realization of what existence is and what it is for? Or does this action, thought or speech set a bend or limitation in the wheel that will cause it to go in circles?

Dharma is intention involving will. Dharma is to flow into intention with will. Dharma is the choice of a being to use their faculties of will, intention, thought, speech and action, a choice to set one's life course this way or not.

Let us oppose the word dharma with non-dharma: casualness, inattention, not building consciousness of what is created and where it's going, not seeing the bigger picture, the future, not paying attention to what came out of the past into the present. It is living in a casualness, a sleep or a semi-sleep. It is feeling that nothing is in your hands, that all is being done to you and for you and around you, that everything that impacts your life is something that was done by others which you had no influence over, and you are just a result of or experiencing the results of. That is not dharmic thought or dharmic belief. That is unconscious thought. It sets the wheel in great circles that will stay within a certain territory for a long time and never move forth from it.

      That is non-dharma and dharma. Consider them both. Non-dharma is not paying attention, not seeking, or even not caring. It is not being a student committed to freedom, non-suffering, true beingness and realization. Dharma *is* being a student of true realization and carrying one's being forward into that realization that everything is an outcome of what has been created, that one continues to be a part of all their experiences. Be patient, then, that ones experiences in the present may well have been created by an unconsciousness in the past. And yet move forward into greater and greater consciousness so that what is being created now will bring a fruitfulness and loveliness in the future.

Patience With The Process

Patience with the dharmic process is imperative. There is no place for judgment. Speaking of dharma and non-dharma is not an invitation to judgment. It is simply a format for looking at what is. Is it dharmic? Does it have the intentions of moving straighter and truer into a light-filled consciousness or not? If you see that it is not, it is still not an invitation to judgment. It is simply an observation of a stage of what is, and it presents a very beautiful, powerful choice. When you know you have a choice, you are beginning to move into the empowerment of divine identity. You have a choice to create greater expansion and freedom, or not. Dharma is the key. Dharma is spiritual action. It is the key to guide one's being towards this greater and greater beauty.

We wish to speak of two levels of being. There is an outer level which is to be considered as the outside, or tread, of the wheel. This is the level of action, of doing, of outer being manifesting, embodying, and carrying forth in one's life and lives. The second level of being is to be likened to the hub, the core of the wheel, with the radiating spokes like the lines of communication between the outer dharmic beingness and the inner beingness or presence, the eternal core of one's soul. To be aware of your being at these two different levels is very useful, so that even thought is this outer rim of the wheel – what you think, feel, do, say, what you feel in your heart-body, what emotions pass through your sky, what thoughts pass through your mind, and what encourages you to speak and share. Listen to what you have said. This is all the dharmic level, the outer level of being that engages with a life and a world, creating cause and effect, setting a course.

The inner level of being is silence, a pure awareness. It is unworded; it is behind thought. It is pure experience of presence. It is an *I AM* that does not have the boundaries of just your being, a place that merges with all beingness. It is the eternal placement of presence and consciousness, a vast sea of light and wisdom - the endless, deepest source of truth, rightness, beauty, and freedom.

Paint within your mind now this wheel, its spokes, rim, and hub, and see that hub as the simple presence of beingness. Or label it: the endless source of light, or God, in all its entirety, or a soul that merges to all souls. Then see the spokes, the streams of consciousness moving into manifestation, into self, egoic presence, character, named beings and all the forms of all beings, which is the rim. The spokes feed and stream back and forth. How many spokes are actively illuminated in your wheel? Indeed, the greater the number and fluency of these spokes, the stronger the wheel, the more exact the circular rim and the straighter the direction. The spokes are the avenues towards manifestation.

Be aware of your being on these two levels, for to have dharmic thought in the first place means that it must arise from the innermost hub and flow through the spokes into mind, which can then carry the print, the track of divine thought, of truth-filled thinking. The source, the sea, must flow through its streams out into creation.

So then the two levels of being require two actions, so to speak, or two places of attention. First one is to sit and allow one's self to melt, merge, and move into the core, the hub beyond self, name, action and position, and exist in greater and greater ease in the pure nature of all beings. This is a meditative action, the expansive consciousness moving beyond self and character, beyond all dharma into the true meaning and source of dharma. Sit there and resource, merge, listen deeply to allow all thought, all will and all one's life's actions to be guided from the hub.

This, then, is how right thought, speech and action come about more easily. It is not about confusion, bantering and struggling with, "Is this or that right?" It isn't the mind, will or emotion that is trying. It is an invitation into the source of all beingness, the God within, the bank of wisdom, the Akashic truth, to flow down the spoke, entering mind, consciousness, and action. Consider this meditative sitting as an immersion into what *is*, giving one's time to just simple immersion, as though polishing the spokes and clearing the streams, breathing into it and finding that it is you, it was you all along, the source of all that you are and all that is.

Sit immersed in the great peace. Then move to the outer level, and feel the connection, the linking of this to that and that to this, so that when one is challenged by another person, or is struggling to find how to be in this most difficult world, it isn't far to reach into the source of truth and let it arise into mind.

What is channelling, this word that implies receiving from beyond one's self? All that really means is having the spokes streaming full and clear from the hub to the rim. It is a well-directed wheel, circular, moving straight and true, so that whenever it comes to an obstacle, it doesn't crash unconsciously but is able to move easily into the source of direction, of all-understanding, and know which way to go.

Channelling, then, is to be thought of as an internal process where one is accessing All-being within one's own being. It is not to be complicated and given many different names. It is simply hearing, speaking, and receiving from the endless source of pure love and truth.

Let us put that word channelling aside. Let us put division aside and let us see who we really are. We are *all that*. We are the outer rim, the spokes and the hub. We are a beauty of beingness on outer and inner levels of description. On the inner level, which is essentially wordless, it is a great expanse of light and presence of love. It can carry all names or no name. On the outer level, it is of unique, distinct character. It is an artistry of consciousness, a musician of sound, a great scientist of understanding. The outer rim is an exquisite manifestation of pure light in all its myriad forms and names. When we use the word "dharma" in light of this description, we say - *Dharma is opening the streams, the spokes of movement, the flow, the channelling of light, truth and the greatest meaning of existence from source to manifestation so that one's works in a lifetime are works that are of love, that create more and more possibility of freedom, peace and realization for oneself and for all. One's actions throughout the days are towards this end.*

That, then, is dharma.

The Middle Path

The Buddha's students came from many different backgrounds. Ananda and Devadatta, his cousins, left behind wealth and social position; Shariputra, Maudgalyayana, and Kashyapa were ascetics won over to the Buddha's path. Upali had been a barber in Kapilavastu. And Sona, also from a wealthy family, had entertained hopes of being a musician, for he loved to play the vina.

When Sona took to the spiritual life, he did so with such zeal that he decided everything else must be thrown overboard. Despite wild animals and poisonous snakes, he went off into the forest alone to practice meditation - and to undo the softness of his pampered past, he insisted on going barefoot.

After some time of this the Buddha decided to go after him. The path was not hard to find, for it was stained with blood from Sona's feet. In addition to his begging bowl, the Blessed One brought something unusual: a vina, whose strings he had loosened until they were limp as spaghetti.

He found Sona meditating under a banyan tree. The boy limped over to greet him, but the Buddha did not seem to notice. All he said was, "Sona, can you show me how to make music with this?"

Sona took the instrument respectfully and fingered a few notes. Then he began to laugh. "Blessed One," he said," you can't produce music when the strings are so loose!" "Oh, I see. Let me try again." And he proceeded to wind the strings so tightly that Sona winced. When the Buddha tested them, all that came out was high-pitched squeaks.

"Blessed One, that won't work either. You'll break the strings. Here, let me tune it for you." He loosened the strings gently, and played a little haunting song.

Then he stopped, for the music brought memories he was afraid to awaken. "It has to be tuned just right to make music," he said abruptly, handing the vina back to the Buddha. "Neither too tight nor too loose. Just right."

"Sona," the Buddha replied," it is the same for those who seek Nirvana. Don't let yourself be slack, but don't stretch yourself to breaking either. The middle course, lying between too much and too little, is the way of my Eightfold Path."

Dhammapada

Practicing Truth

We would speak now on the practical manner in which one would move from a non-dharmic life into a dharmic life. How can one engage one's consciousness into these things? What are some practical ways that you shift unconscious, casual beingness into conscious, directed beingness? We have spoken over and over of meditation being a primary action in bringing one closer and closer to the source, where one is becoming more conscious of the eternal centre. Soul begins to be able to stream into one's presence and mind.

Meditation is truly a very fundamental, practical practice towards what we are speaking of. Meditation is intending to exist in the expansiveness of one's being and to move one's consciousness out of the mind and emotion into the soul, the presence that does not die. Mind and emotion will die. The character that is developed within a lifetime will die. The truth, presence, lessons, and deepening that that character has obtained will not die. All of that is absorbed into the soul and taken into the deeper character, the true nature, and the essential beingness. Meditation is choosing to be in that essential beingness, choosing to move one's point of awareness from the limited corner of mind and emotional nature into this presence. It creates an ease of movement from outer rim to inner hub. Indeed, it creates an entire spoke, a streaming link between that which is eternal and that which is temporary.

To meditate in a practice is to change one's identity. It is to identify with one's life from the hub, from the essential beingness. It is to move one's identity from being lodged in mind and what it thinks, emotion and what it feels, and will and what it wills. In short, it is an expansion of one's identity from a temporary, illusory self - illusory in that it is always changing and is unaware of the eternal nature, the stream of lives and the doctrine of oneness.

The mind can perceive the doctrine of oneness, but the doctrine of oneness is not experienced within mind. The emotional self can actually experience the doctrine of oneness and yet the emotional self is at the whim of will and mind and is often cramped and crippled and hurting, trying to protect the separate self that arises from mind and will. Meditative practice, then, gives the emotional self a greater source from which to sit, feeling into the great oneness, peace, and love. Meditative practice gives mind a chance to expand, to grasp much greater concepts and move beyond the limitations of what self is, giving mind an even greater journey to explore. It also gives it a chance to rest and simply watch.

<u>Mind in its most peaceful state simply watches</u>. It does not think; it simply, purely perceives, like a window that is wiped crystal clean and just allows the light to move back and forth.

A meditative practice gives the will a chance to engage itself along dharmic paths, for the will is a soldier, truly, just a servant. When given a task it will carry it out to the bitter end, a soldier that has been sent to go here and there, to crash this door down and to dig that ditch. The will is a worker bee. Who commands the will, then? Does the will receive its commands from a limited self, or from the expansive Self? From the emotions that are trying to protect the illusory separate self, or from the emotion that feels the great peace and oneness? Meditation is a skill that moves one from here to there and opens the spokes from hub to rim. It is most practical and most profound.

Teachings
On Meditation

Meditation is the royal road leading straight to the centre, opening the being most directly, leading through mind, emotion, and will to the eternal nature. Door after door is opened through meditation, until there are no doors left and one sits in the light-filled plane of their true being. The true being is that which does not die and that which is not separate from grace, from omniscient truth. Meditation is the key to each door, each room that must be passed through until the room without walls is entered.

What is meditation? It is a personal practice whereby one learns to quiet and still the mind, emotion, character and self. One learns through various techniques to re-educate the consciousness into expansion. It is the format and setting for this redirecting of the mind and self. Meditation is a practice where one becomes more and more comfortable and skilled at going into stillness, into the inner being, into listening, realizing, and attending to what one is hearing and feeling. It is an inner dialogue and reception where growth in consciousness can actually occur.

Meditation requires sitting, letting go of the outer layers of interaction, turning one's focus and intention into the inner planes, readdressing the outer and what is heard, learning how the outer world stimulates the consciousness, and becoming aware of the triggers and responses. In short, meditation is the royal road to consciousness. It is entering into consciousness, deepening it, claiming it, becoming it.

Meditation is goal-less, in the ordinary sense, yet it can also be described in terms of goals. It is goal-less in that the practice and intention itself is the fulfilment. Sitting in meditation and watching the busyness of the mind, or the pain in the heart and anguish in the emotion, is significant. To watch is to step slightly apart from and observe and notice what is there. The business of the mind is like traffic on a highway or street. In meditation, one steps aside and watches rather than trying to find a vehicle and enter into the stream of traffic. The awareness from within the busyness is much smaller than the awareness from without.

It is the same with the emotional being and pain, anguish, and feelings. One steps away so that the whole shape, voice, and progression can be seen. There is no perspective from the inside, which is filled with pain and feeling, with no whole shape or understanding.

That alone is a success in meditation, to be able to notice and watch what is within one's being, whether it is in one's mind or feelings or perhaps in the body if it is in pain. It is watching the pain without going into anguish, judgment, or rejection of the body, just watching and noticing what the body has, listening to it speaking through its pain, listening to the emotion: what is it saying?

Meditation is stepping apart in order to have a better view, a greater perspective, standing on a hill so one can see the vista of one's being and watch from where something comes from to where it is going, seeing the patterns of its passage through the plain below. One can see what caused a feeling to arise and what thoughts and perhaps what physical pain it led to.

Meditation is a grand perspective of the wise, like a lord looking over his territory and seeing what this group of people over here is doing and how it is affecting that group of people over there. In order to manage the territory, the lord must have a view of the whole. Meditation is learning to be the lord within one's being, to see the whole territory and how one aspect or thought is affecting another. It is seeing an interconnectedness, that it is all a whole and it all affects the whole so that one activity in one corner of the territory does not go without being felt throughout the entire land, and the actions of one people here will affect the others or the river or the forest.

Meditation, then, is seeing the interconnectedness of the whole being, how emotions arose from thoughts, and thoughts arose from fears and misunderstandings, and physical illness arose from emotion that may have been carried for too long, or from consciousness that never surfaced - the suppression of awareness. The royal road of meditation leads straight up to the highest hill with the greatest view of the territory.

There is effort on this road. One must learn each step that goes higher into greater perspective, in a sense removing oneself from the centre of interactions in one corner of the territory, where one can get lost and no longer see what is occurring anywhere else. One can get lost in their emotions and conclusions and not see anything else, or get lost in their physical illness and see it as unrelated to anything else. Each step upwards gives more perspective, unity, and expansiveness.

Therefore there *is* a goal to meditation. It is to have the greatest view and understanding possible of what one's existence is, who one's being is, and what one's purpose is. None of this can be seen unless one is truly becoming the lord of one's own territory. Then one can see and understand the past, present and future - how the past led to the present, where it is all going, and how to manage all the qualities of one's being so that the future brings more peace.

Consider this very powerful statement – how the past led to the present and how the present will lead to the future. This is in your hands. You are the creator. Meditation is a tool of awareness, so that one can take this more and more into one's hands and create peace and unity. One leaves the valley of unconsciousness, of apparent victim-hood, and climbs to the hilltop where one is in command and can see what happened, what happens and what could happen.

From the hilltop, then, what does the lord do? Does he stay there? No, he must go down into the valley over and over again and instruct and teach and guide, building consciousness within all the parts, all the peoples, linking and teaching them, "When you do this, it happens this way over there. So do that so that all will benefit." The lord must be very active, making many journeys into the valley of separation to unify and draw together so that all are conscious of each other and working in unity.

The lord of your consciousness must also enter into mind, emotion, and will to teach and instruct. The mind must realize where thoughts and beliefs lead, especially when acted on. The mind must see where the beliefs arose.

The emotional being, like a beautiful child, must learn what emotion does, how it fills the entire landscape, like a weather system, with sun or rain, devastation or nurturing. The emotional being must learn its place, must learn to respond to wisdom and be used to love, not to be angry or to reject or react.

The will, the little foot soldiers down there in the valley that are so busy, taking messages here and there, ordering people to do this and that – the will especially needs to be taken by its shoulders and spoken to and taught, "This is what must be created! Do this for that!" The will must be taught by the lord - the higher awareness and greater perspective that has seen the whole - so that the foot solider is building towards the future and unity. The little foot soldiers of the will would just as easily serve one demanding protection or crying in anguish and blaming another. The will doesn't care. It will do whatever it's asked. Therefore let the lord of your being instruct the will.

The lord – what is this? This is your true being before, during, and after, the indescribable mergence of your being to all beings, the God flowing within you. Meditation then, door by door, stage by stage, is building a consciousness of this god-being that you are, giving more and more rulership and dominion to it so that the landscape of the human self is acting in unity with truth and building peace within the world.

This, then, is the goal of meditation. Meditation is the tool for conscious development, the royal road to consciousness. We speak of it as a practical tool so that it may be chosen, for what is the use of expansive descriptions of truth with no way of understanding how to attain? Meditation is the tool to attain this consciousness, to learn to position the aspects of the being so that they are in the right configuration: the soul being lord; the mind being the receiver of information, the perceiver and brilliant articulate manifestation of divine information; the emotion being that which gives love, feels compassion, knows truth, embraces and nurtures; the will being simply the force, the executor, that which builds paths, creates structures, waters gardens; the body encapsulates the being into a world, a sphere of activity and evolution; the body is the dancer, the movement and the anchor. Having the aspects of one's being in the harmonious configuration of their purpose, with the captain and the supreme wisdom flowing through all - meditation is the tool towards this.

Through meditation, on many levels from the simplest to the most sublime, one evolves. Meditation engages the use of breath, deeply and slowly, filling the cellular body fully with oxygen, which is the primary nutrient for the cellular body. As each nerve cell receives oxygen, it becomes at peace. As each brain cell, indeed *every* cell within the body, receives oxygen, it becomes attuned and toned to its purpose, and is not craving or desperate, at loss or suffering. Deep and slow breath fills the cellular body with oxygen, bringing calm, stability, and health - the smallest benefit then to the physical plane of being.

The breath, as it soothes and stills the nervous system, soothes and stills the mind. The mind is a force field of impulses; thoughts dart across like messages down a nerve path. The mind becomes highly active and chaotic, and can have firings of nerve pulse through it chaotically, nonsensically, some creating fear, some creating confusion. The mind is a complex force field. The deep, slow breath slows these impulses, slows the activity of the nervous system of the mind and as it goes into peace and stillness, greater awareness can flood in.

Greater awareness does not use the same nerve paths as thought, conjecture, deduction, criticism, judgment, or fear. It sits not just in mind but also in heart, in every sense, filling and surrounding, like a sky through and within at all times. As the force field becomes calmer, stiller, more receptive and crystalline, higher, pristine exquisite awareness arrives. Deep, slow breath is the medium for stilling the mind and nervous system and learning to control and settle the chaos of mind's action.

The beginning, then, of meditation is this: learning the depth of breath, being content to watch the body infill and out, slow and deep, watching the nervous system and mind become as calm as a still lake. Ripples of thought can be watched, some taken note of, others let go. The breath is a golden key. It is far more than just a physical process of bringing oxygen to the cellular body, for our consciousness is breath-mediated within this body, brain and complex nervous system. Therefore breath and consciousness are highly related. Without breath there is no consciousness in this body. With right use of breath, there is tremendous consciousness in this body.

Therefore consider the importance of breath. Be aware of how you breathe. Shallow, erratic breath creates shallow, erratic thought, consciousness, experience, and sometimes pain and anguish. Shallow, erratic breath creates illness, for the body is not receiving enough oxygen. It can create headaches and limitations in many ways. Deep, full breath does the opposite, bringing the forerunner of all other nutrients to the cells. Oxygen is needed by every metabolic process, nerve interaction, nutrient uptake and organ response. It is the primary nutrient for your being on all levels.

Consider the importance of breath and be aware of how you breathe. Simply by learning true, deep, meditative breath, you can change your being towards awareness, wholeness, calm and health.

Once the calmness and the stillness of mind and emotion have been learned and the breath has become quiet and still, breath is a passage towards learning the expansiveness and true possibilities of awareness. Once one is sitting in the stillness and calm of the meditative state, the breath becomes quiet and soft. The body becomes profoundly still and the consciousness sits lightly within. The metabolism becomes very slow. There are those that have learned this meditative state who hardly breathe, who sit for astounding lengths of time without food or water. The human being is capable of this. This is not being spoken of as a goal, but to teach that consciousness within you can move to such an expansion and yet still be housed ever so lightly within the physical form.

The peace and equanimity of a being in the meditative state is profound and has been measured. It affects the entire being, bringing harmony, health, and longevity to every cell and organ. Therefore the benefits of meditation can be purely towards physical health, calm, and learning to live free of stress.

Meditation, as we said, is a room without walls, a vast plain of light. Those who sit barely breathing are not meditating for physical health or stress relief. They have entered into the all-beingness, the god-nature, the highest capacity of consciousness - nirvana.

Also we would say this is not your goal; this is the goal of that one who sits there. What is *your* goal? Take not the goal of any other. Let it be suggested that your goal be towards health, peace, happiness, joy and wellbeing to whatever level that means for you.

Meditation is a spiritual tool, the royal road to true awareness. Through meditation one can attune into what God is, what divine wisdom would say. One can solve the world's problems. This is being said with a smile. How simple to sit in stillness and understand the answer, rather than meetings and discussions, minds chipping away at the mountain of the human condition and its problems. To sit in stillness and listen – *be still and know that I am God* - for beyond mind, character and self, the divine knowledge is yours. It is meant to flow into your being and manifest in this world. Therefore let the one, perhaps, who sits without breathing for years begin to breath again and stand up and take the truth into the communities and serve.

This, too, is the goal of meditation: to learn how to live truthfully, in service to the best in humanity, bringing about the best action, finding one's way around every corner, through every maze, problem and difficulty. No meetings, or trying to decipher the issue with mind, but going into meditation and listening to divine source and hearing what is the best way forward.

Therefore meditation is an active tool towards manifesting rightness within the world. It is a way of linking the centre of the dharmic wheel to the rim where the print is left in the soil, the direction is chosen and the way is carved.

How does one meditate? Meditation, it must be said, has been practiced and taught by many peoples, religions, and paths throughout the world. Therefore it has many names, ways, and teachers. This is fortunate, but confusing. This is a rich landscape. You may turn in many directions to receive the ways, forms, the sangha, community, and fellowship of meditation. Truly it is for you to find that which matches your being at this time. How intensively are you prepared to move into the stillness? How strict a form do you wish to undertake? What do you want the form of your meditation to be associated with? What teacher, atmosphere, and ambience? This is all your beautiful journey of discovery.

Gautama Buddha is the king, the master teacher of meditation. It was through meditation and sitting, persisting in stilling the force field of mind until he found the brilliance and entered the true nature, the Buddhic field, the awakened state. The Buddha did not sit in this lovely state of awakening and enjoy it. Rather, he sat and developed a method of teaching until it was clear and intact, and then began a ministry. The Buddha, then, is an ultimate teacher of the form of meditation that leads to true realization of all-beingness. Even within Buddhism there are many forms. There have been many buddhas since, Buddha meaning 'awakened one', and many teachers who have developed followings.

Be aware that all are speaking of the same principles, values, and goals, though perhaps cloaking them with different experiences, languages, countries, and needs of different peoples throughout time. Do not be confused. Sense with your heart and being what teaches you, what speaks to you. Consider the Buddha. Examine the teachings, their beauty and simplicity. The Buddha has followings in many different countries and you will find the forms of meditative practice as different as the many forms of the Buddha statues.

    We would like to put the word meditation aside and call it something else: inner stillness, attunement, listening to God, the path of prayer and stillness. The Christ did not use the word meditation, nor was it the method that he spoke of. And yet in the wilderness, where his being broke through into greater awareness of truth and awakened, it was the same dynamics of moving inward, opening door after door with greater and greater attention and mindfulness, meeting every voice that came up, every devil, threat, limitation, and boundary, breathing through them, reaching through until the awakened being emerged. The forty days in the desert: what was that? Consider it. It was a passage like the Buddha's sitting and moving inward, disengaging from the world, from the activity of mind and emotion until the soul was listened to and heard. Therefore in Christianity, the word meditation may just mean thoughtfulness or may mean something quite different. Don't get caught in the words. Call it what you will: inner attunement, sitting with breath, or just sitting.

    We would teach here of a form of meditation that may be tried and considered. We will speak of different forms of meditation so that a practical choice of methods is given here. The body and the being is a creature of habit. Therefore, create a habit, place, position, and situation that can be returned to repeatedly, making it easier and familiar and developing an ease of entry into the meditative state. Find a place within your home, a cushion or a bench that is comfortable and allows your back to sit straight and true. Find the silent time of the day or music that assists you. Find then a repetitive pattern that can teach your body, mind, emotion and entire being to know what to expect, so that you enter in more easily, not creating resistance or feeling strange in this place, or uncomfortable on this new cushion, listening with interest to the music, getting distracted by a myriad of things. Create a meditative or inner attunement habit.

  This, then, is an outer provision for meditation. There can be more than one. You may find a group that you are comfortable with. But always find a personal place and time within your home that is used continually, letting your body find an ease and strength in a straight spine. The straightness of the spine is an alertness and a signal to your whole being that you are moving into greater awareness. To slump with the spine is to choose lesser awareness. To sit with the spine erect, straight and true towards the sun and the sky is to choose greater awareness. As the body is repeatedly treated this way, moving into the straight spine with ease on the proper height of cushion, awareness is instantly begun to be entered and chosen.

  Address the first part of the meditation towards position and softness in any muscle group, any place in the body where it can be - the face, jaw, shoulders, and belly. Realize the tension that you are holding in your shoulders, face or belly is attached to a thought or previous feeling that will lead you away from this moment.

This first phase of meditation is to relax entirely into this moment, letting there be no other moment ahead that you're moving towards, or a moment behind that is pulling you back. To realize the full awareness within this moment one must relax into it. First, then, physically see where the tension is that is holding you backwards and gearing you forwards.

Then choose and learn the breath that enters deep, moving down into the belly and letting the diaphragm drop. The belly is soft and expansive and then the breath enters the chest, filling the lower and upper lobes completely, slowly, in one great stream. Enjoy and feel the depth of breath and how the lungs desire and long for this full breath. Let the entire body enjoy and engage in this full experience of breath. Learn to breathe so that each breath is an experience of fullness and depth from the belly and the root right up until the very brain is filled and charged with lovely, light-filled breath after breath of increasing slowness, depth, and brilliance, watching with delight how it claims and expands you, stills your racing heart, soothes the pain and relieves the tension that you may be feeling in your belly or chest. The breath is the ultimate medicine for tension or pain.

Actively, then, learn the deep, light-filled sparkling breath. Imagine it entering your whole body, filling every cell, corner, blood vessel and every region of brain. This beginning phase of meditation – give it time. It is primary and foundational. Remember we are teaching you one form of meditation and you may find others. This one is being taught through the writer as is taught to the groups on a weekly basis. The breath, then, is learned from the inside, entered like a great stream of life and light.

The mind and emotions will enter in because that is what they do. What to do then? Let the breath surround the thoughts and feelings like a wind surrounds leaves floating in the sky, like it surrounds everything in its path. The breath is bigger, boundary-less. Thought is concrete, darting, moving through the atmosphere, and feeling also has shape. Let the breath surround and penetrate and do not struggle. Let the thought or feeling be there. Do not push away or engage in struggle with any part of your being. Realize it is there for a reason. The heart perhaps needs to speak and the mind is used to speaking. The mind wasn't finished speaking when you sat down, of course. Watch what it speaks, watch what is felt, and yet do not engage with it. Just watch. Let the breath continue to be deep and pure and surround the thought and with the exhale let the thought be carried away.

A key to successful meditation is not struggling, but to yield and allow this moment to be what it is. In this moment there is this thought and feeling. There is that great tremendous sound outside of my room. Watch it, allow it, and continue to breath as you allow life to be just what it is in this moment, within and without.

As your mind, emotions, and will learn that you are not going to struggle or fight, they relax, they let go, they don't need to push their way in and say, "Let me have a place here, I need to be part of this!" They learn that they *are* a part of this. Like if a child who wanted to come in on a conversation of adults was not sent out but given a knee to sit on, and then the child became bored with the conversation and left. The child was not told they didn't have a place, and so didn't need to push and struggle for one. It is the same with the mind – let it be there until it is not interested anymore and leaves. Let the emotion be there until it feels it doesn't need to be and the stillness and calm are there instead.

 The key, then, to meditation is yielding, allowing, and being present with each breath and moment. This stillness is the beginning of the practice of meditation, learning to use the breath to assist one in being present and learning to be in a different relationship with mind, emotion, and will that allows them to be there and yet gives no energy or focus.

 Once the mind and character of self learn to relax and have less interruption, there begins to be the experience of expansion, an accessing and realizing of the greater nature - atma. This phase of meditation can also be difficult, where the person panics or fears the expansiveness and can feel disoriented, dizzy and have many strange sensations of floating, sinking, becoming extremely heavy or weightless. The person in their panic of disorientation may begin to have wild thoughts and images and even begin to feel delusion.

 This phase of meditation may require guidance, or that you reach out for help. Yet if you orient yourself to breath and breathe deeply and slowly through it, knowing where you're headed - you want only peace, only truth, only the highest form of consciousness that is filled with light and simplicity. By holding the intention and persisting with slow, deep breath, this phase of disorientation is mastered.

This phase can be where one stops in meditation and does not know how to go through, and yet this is where the expansion is understood. The identity of atma, of greater nature, becomes experienced, and the identity of the being begins to truly change. One realizes they are not just "Jean" or "Susan"; they are not just the named self or lifetime or their emotions or thoughts or profession – they are not the role of the human being. One's identity moves beyond all that.

It is a time when it can be frightening and confusing. Well, then, who am I? Let the question resound for the answer is profound – who am I? Meditation leads farther into this experience of true beingness, of knowing you are all, feeling at one, as though breathing within all. Meditation leads one into the truth of all-beingness, of no separation. Sit with your meditation, wherever it leads you, taking it a little farther by staying with your breath, and if need be, engaging in thoughts that direct and guide.

Constant repeating of the Holy Name is more than praise, at length the voice will sink to silent repetition in the Heart, and in this way is meditation learnt.

Better than meditation that recurs in broken fits and starts is that which is a steady ceaseless flow, like to the course of falling oil, or a perennial stream.

The Poems of Ramana Maharshi

Inner Guidance Thoughts & Mantras

*A*llowing the mind to be teacher and guide is a very successful way to view the journey into the meditative state, understanding that the pure state has very little thought within it and the mind is quite still. And yet the mind can be used on the way. As the mind is trained to assist the inner state to be reached, it learns its place in the balance of mind, emotion, will, and character in relationship to soul and true nature.

Many statements can be creatively found that assist the mind towards meditation. Statements that are often taught in guided meditation are simple sentences, such as - *All that I am is breathing. All that I am is present. All that I am is watching.* Let these words travel slowly along the breath, especially the word *'all'*, letting its true meaning be entered. Let the words *'I am'* sit slowly within the breath and be felt into. Whatever the ending of the sentence is, be fully present with the meaning of it. What does it mean for your whole being to be present? How does it feel for your whole being to breathe, to listen? The sentence is powerful, simple, and profound if it is deeply listened to and entered.

Use the guidance sentence repeatedly for a time during meditation to assist the consciousness towards full presence or absolute listening. Use it towards total awareness of the breath. Use the sentence repeatedly, slowly, in and out of the breath, until the experience is full of presence, of listening or breathing. Use the sentence slowly along the breath, letting *'All that I am'* come on the very slow in-breath, and the sentencing ending such as *'is listening'*, or *'is breathing'*, to reside in the out-breath, allowing there to be a silent time at the end of the out-breath where the meaning of the sentence is felt.

It has been taught that to breath slowly is to create longevity in the body. To breath rapidly is to live for less years, speeding the metabolism, taxing the system. To breath slowly is to create a deep, harmonious, sustainable physical form. To allow the sentence, then, to be fully experienced can also encourage slow breathing, taking a very long in-breath, feeling the words *'All that I am'* slowly playing themselves out, like the verses of a song travelling on a note, and resting into the out-breath as though concluding a sentence. Each breath, each inhale and exhale, is a complete sentence. There is no need to be anything else. What else could be said after *'All that I am is present'* or, *'All that I am is listening'*? After the sentence is said, it is just being present, just experiencing what is being listened to.

Consider the profound nature of using mind towards inner guidance during meditation. There are other statements in this amazing ability of language that can be used in meditation: *'Breathing in, breathing out'*. Let the mind instruct the process.

Soham, a Sanskrit word that means *'I am that'*. Soham is considered to be the sound of the breath. *'So'* is the in-breath, *'ham'* the out-breath, as though with every breath your being is saying, "I am that", as though breath is speaking a language, a constant reminding and telling - *I am that*. Soham can be chosen as syllables to be used along the breath, knowing the meaning or not, or using the English meaning – *'I am'* on the in-breath, *'that'* on the out-breath.

What does *'I am that'* mean? If you listen into the words, into the silence of breath, *'All that I am'* shall unfold experientially. If the mind is busy alongside of the Soham breath, *'I am that'* is all the busyness. If the senses are gathering what is being heard outside, *'I am that'* is all that is being heard outside, for you are a part of all. If you have entered in the stream of pure awareness, *'I am that'* is this stream.

'I am that', then, is a meditative inner thought that powerfully brings you into the moment, not rejecting anything about the moment but engaging fully with all that is in it. *'I am the moment and all that is in it'*.

Light – use the concept and words for light or love interchangeably. *'I am the light'*. Breathe light in and out, feeling the meaning of *'I am light'*.

We are not here to give great, exhaustive descriptions of what light is. We are asking you to *find* what light is. Light is an electric bulb, a candle flame, the sun. This is the light that comes to the physical eyes and is experienced and labelled as light within the brain. What else is light? You will find light and its meaning as you claim it and identify with it within your being, heart, and breath.

What is divine light? Is that the candle flame, sun, or light bulb? What is divine radiance? What is the effulgence of the omniscient master? What is the halo that is seen around the enlightened ones? What is the greater description and meaning of light? Take that into the meditation simply by breathing light. Breathing in and breathing out are prefixes to meditative inner guidance laws, such as breathing in *'I am light'*, breathing out *'I am peace'*, or breathing in *'I listen'*, breathing out *'I watch'*.

These are suggestions of inner guidance thoughts, not to be said lightly like a sentence that runs through the mind but the deeper, full meaning entered into. Using the prefix *'breathing in'* or *'breathing out'* constantly gathers the awareness to the breath and to the exact, subtle, and distinct moment of the present. It is a tool for gathering the consciousness, and once it has been gathered into this process of being in the moment, the need to use sentences and thoughts that guide melts away. One is just breathing in and listening and breathing out and being light. It heralds the experience and the mind is to be used to prepare the territory for consciousness.

The mind is not the territory. It is the preparer of the territory. It is the messenger. The mind is the John the Baptist, the one who precedes the state that is being described. And yet this state is experienced beyond mind, through the whole being and beyond being. Using the mind to give inner guidance thoughts is using it most appropriately towards spiritual development.

We speak of the Buddhist practice of *'metta'* – loving kindness meditation or compassionate practice, using the mind actively to repeat, "May all beings be at peace. May all beings find happiness", letting those metta thoughts travel and direct the breath into the heart and out. This trains one to be compassionate, to consider and hold all beings in prayer and hope that they deserve and may receive happiness and peace.

Metta is a branch of inner guidance meditation with a distinct goal towards sitting in the practice or experience of compassion and lifting one's being from despair, disregard, criticism and judgment into expansion and equality, developing unity and addressing life from a place of compassion. This meditation is an active use of mind and heart towards developing and emanating love. What you exist and build within your being, you emanate without. Metta is a training, a shaping of consciousness of the heart and mind towards compassion and love.

Loka somasta sukinombavantu – Sanskrit for *'May all beings in this world find peace and be happy'* - so simple, this sentence. It is a mantra, repeated over and over. Why is something repeated? The western mind balks heartily at repetition, feeling as though it is being pulled into a place it does not want to go. Where is it being pulled? It is being pulled deeper into the meaning of the words, for the mind can look at them and say, "Oh I get it, I understand, ok, now what?" But the meaning of the words is far deeper than the mind can appreciate. Remember, mind only prepares the way, organizes the words, comprehends them to some extent. But the mind is becoming accustomed to thinking it has the whole picture. Once the words are organized and the comprehension is there, it wants to move on.

But no, wait. What is the deeper meaning of *'May all beings in this worlds be happy'*? Is it everybody just laughing, not having concerns and worries? Listen deeply in the act of repetition. Consciousness begins to explode, to widen and fill in, so that the true meaning is felt and known. The simple mantra of metta can bring you through everything - all the resistance you have that would judge, all the, "You should be happy but maybe not *you*. You deserve happiness but why should that one? You have created happiness by all the wonderful things you do, but you've done nothing over here, so why should you have happiness?"

The mantra is repeated until the truth is seen and known that all beings are essentially one, there is no being that does not deserve happiness, and no being that is not aimed and directed with their entire creation and purpose towards peace. No being exempt from grace – none. There is no being with judgment held upon it by God or whatever term one might give the almighty presence that says, "You can enter the kingdom of heaven but not *you*." There is no division such as this within creation.

Repeating the mantra of metta helps the wisdom of unity enter into your being, so that as you walk through your days you don't exist in the subtle and silent criticism and judgment of those who have more or less, deserve more or less of your love, attention and consideration. Do you find yourself raptly listening to one person who may have something of importance to give you, or is respected and considered by others, and therefore you are listening? And you find yourself impatiently waiting for the sentence to end of another who you or others don't respect, who you think has nothing of value to say. Question yourself. The practice of metta helps you listen to both equally.

It is said that the wise are affected not by praise or blame. They live in an equanimity, a unity where all beings are equal. The wise can afford to listen to the one in the street who may ramble as equally as the one who is held high by society. Why? Not because of what is being said, because the rambling may be nonsensical and feel like a waste of time, but because the I's in both ensue from the same source, and the hearts of both need to be listened to and considered as brethren or kin.

This is the teaching and meaning of repetition, not to numb and get lost in it, which can happen as well, but to attend to the meaning of what is being said repeatedly until one begins to experience its.

So we have moved on our speaking here from inner guidance thoughts in the language that you understand to the use of mantra that is often not in English but in Sanskrit or in some other language, which is a very big step to take, repeating words in a language one doesn't know. Even if the translation is given, by listening in to the syllables of the Sanskrit language, you are not understanding with your English speaking mind what is being said. Mantras often are repeating the names of god, in their simplest version, asking for peace, for blessing. The meaning is simplest in aiming and immersing one's consciousness towards the higher truth, the god-nature.

Use the mantras, then, to immerse oneself in God-nature, using them until silence has entered and one is just sitting in the God-nature. This is the meaning, power, and use of mantras, to use the brain in its articulation, its ability to hear, speak, and understand, all for the purpose of experiencing God-nature. *'I am the light'* – that is experiencing the god-nature.

The Aumkara: the ancient, most simple of mantras, which is repeating Aum fully, from A and U to M, letting the syllable sounds travel and vibrate through one's head and being with the silence that follows, singing the all-encompassing name of the whole creation, of God, the Sound which gathers all-beingness into one word – Aum.

This most simple and profound of mantras can fill the consciousness and every cell with the divine presence, non-articulate experience of truth, the Aumkara. Enter into it fully, repeating it, learning how to fully Aum, drawing the A deep from the belly up through the heart, having it move into a U, letting it fill the mind with the M, and letting the lips close on the M and holding in completion of the sound. There are many Sanskrit mantras, which we will not go into and yet hold yourself open to them when the time comes.

The Sanskrit language is the most directly spiritual description in language that can be found, the most ancient, subtle and advanced description of the true nature of soul. It is a study that is fascinating, a practice that is deep. The living master Sathya Sai Baba encourages the use of the *Gayatri* mantra.

Om, Bhuh Bhuwah Suwaha
Tat Savitur Varenyum
Bhargo Devasya Dheemahi
Dhiyo Yo Nah Prachodayat

Om ~ Shanti ~ Shanti ~ Shanti

(Supreme Lord! Creator of the three worlds, past, present and future; Glorious splendour illuminating the three regions of experience, gross, subtle and causal; Radiant Grace flowing from that Light; We meditate on thy divine radiance; We pray for the Grace of thy Illumination within us!)

The Gayatri Mantra

The Gayatri mantra has a sublime, intelligent meaning. We will give the description of it in the way of the Hindi that use the Gayatri mantra. It is to repeatedly use the mantra, sometimes with the japa mala, the 108 prayer beads, saying the Gayatri 108 times, and holding the bead between the thumb and the third finger, repeating it, feeling it, entering it. '108' represents the many forms of God-nature that the Hindi recognize. It is a path, and as Sathya Sai Baba teaches, choose the path that you were born to. Use the path that was given to you and you can feast from any other table as long as it deepens you in your truth.

The Gayatri mantra is India; Sanskrit is India, and India is a spiritual heart of humanity, with a great feast table to give to us. We can use this mantra in the context of who we are. We do not need to be Hindi or sing it 108 times. We can use it from where we sit and from who we are. It is a profound, highly intelligent mantra that evolves light and spiritual intelligence within the being and radiates it to all beings.

In the path of yoga there is an entire branch that is of mantra. In finding the mantra the suits each person, a very personal relationship ensues. Often the mantra is given by a master to a student that is individual, given just to them, a sacred gift, a tool. This is precious and if this is your way, honour it and use it well, and realize that you can also choose a mantra in English, an inner guidance thought in English, that leads you most directly into the experience of peace, grace or divine nature.

Mantra, then, is an ancient use of mind within meditation, using the mind as a continual arena of god-natured thought, that teaches the mind its place and uses its power to prepare the way for the experience of atma, nirvana, expansion, true beingness, and peace.

What are the goals of meditation? We ask this question again. And these words could be lofty or simple. In utter simplicity, it is to be at peace with who you are, in the moment you are in, in the life that you are in, in the day that you are in, in the form that you are in. Soham.

The eternal Atma Tattwa is immanent within us. It can be realized in a moment if you give up Dehabhimana (body attachment) and cultivate Atmabhimana (Atmic consciousness). You think you are the body and develop attachment to it. But how long does this attachment last? So long as the process of inhalation and exhalation continues in the body, you consider it as yours. Once the process comes to a halt, you do not know what is happening around. The human body, though of perishable nature, teaches one great lesson, namely, 'Soham' (That I am).

Sanathan Sarati
March 2004

Choosing To Watch

We continue to speak of practicality, of how to engage a dharmic existence into one's identity and experience one's personal reality in these ways.

There requires an attention and a choice to watch what arises in one's thoughts and to watch what one says. Observe it and its effect, always without judgment. Hold that strongly there – *always without judgment.* Simply watch what has arisen in your thoughts and how it creates feeling. What feeling comes from that thought? What did you notice happened from what you said? This choice to watch is a part of the dharmic practicality where one actually learns and builds experience. Ask, "Is that thought leading to freedom or closure and limitation? Does this thought create peace and love or pain and hurt?" That simple action, to enquire after one's thoughts and follow them, creates a powerful sense of choice. Do I need to continue with that thought? What would be a better, more instructed, higher-action thought? What would lead further into a freedom from this or into a resolution and what would create more opportunities for peace for my being and this being in front of me?

This may sound very internal and so it is. It is having the great single eye of one's being open, watching. You may choose to watch what the speech of others causes in you or in those around you. Watch this.

Learn from it. Realize there is always a choice. If the speech of others caused pain and confusion, there was a choice. It could have been said in a different way or not said at all. Right speech can mean silence. Right action can mean non-action. It is then asking, "Should I speak sometimes or is it best not to? Should I act or is it best not to? What furthers this situation towards love and peace and what does not?" One choosing to exist in dharma asks such questions, giving oneself those moments to ask first before speaking or acting, and giving oneself time to observe what one is thinking and to advise oneself perhaps to find another thought, to access the hub and allow a more truth-filled thought to replace one that may have arisen from will, from a limited, cramped emotional state, or from a fearful mind.

      To hold a journal and to have a practice in writing can be an important way to anchor this process, where one asks these questions on paper and takes the time to examine what the thoughts were, what they created, and opening to what a more healing thought may have been. This is engaged personal reality along a dharmic path.

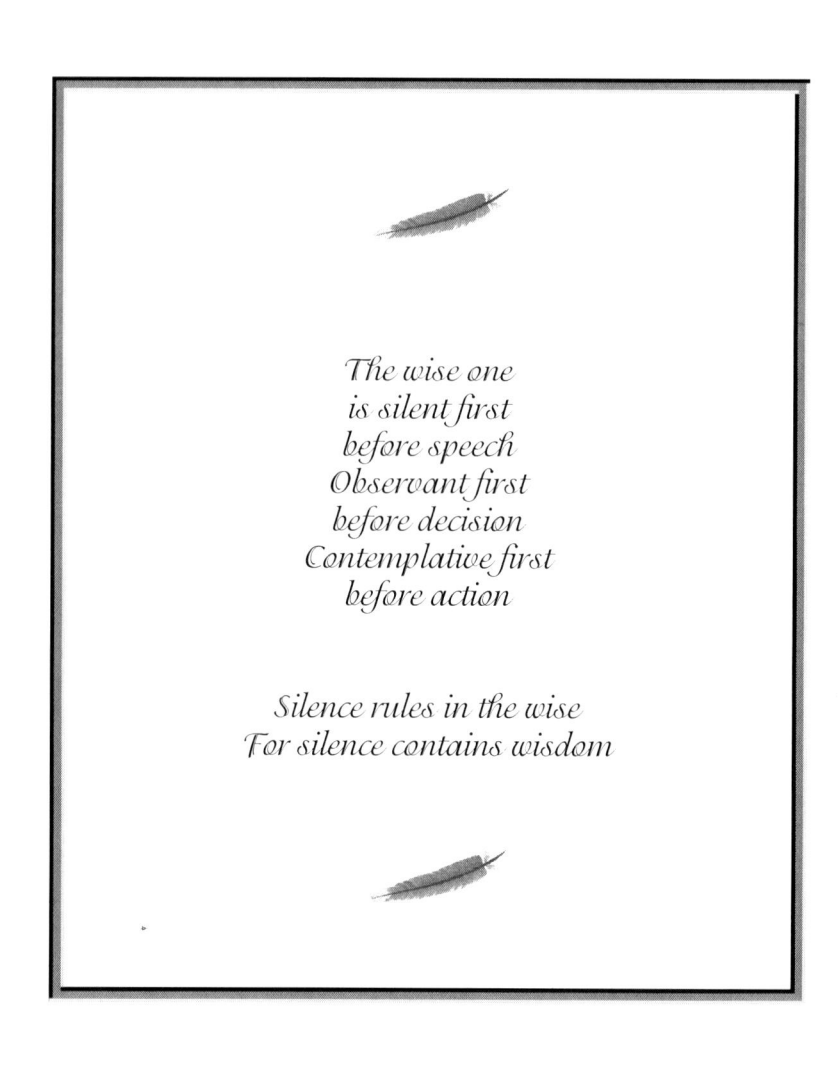

*The wise one
is silent first
before speech
Observant first
before decision
Contemplative first
before action*

*Silence rules in the wise
For silence contains wisdom*

Studying The Great Teachers

To engage one's personal reality is to study and listen to the masters and teachers. There are many masters, teachers, texts and writings that instruct dharmic thought, action, speech and creation. Filling one's mind with the words and actions of these teachers gives pathways for truth to imprint with ease. Studying the teachings and experiences of those that have gone before you and those that have become a fully-illumined dharmic wheel can instruct your being deeply as to *how*. To attend to a teacher or master fully in devotional nature is to allow that example, that illumined wheel, deeper into your own being where it instructs you in a cellular, energetic beyond-mind way.

This, too, is a practical, powerful method of moving oneself into conscious beingness. One can choose to learn from the teachers and masters and even find one particular master who can imprint you closely, who you can fall in love with and draw close to your being. Bringing a being such as this closer to you through your heart, through devotion and immersion in all that they are, prints you with the way, the information and the avenues so that they are traced within your being and are easier to activate. It is still your own choice and your own action that will illumine the spokes and create that light-filled being of *you*. And yet you will not be working in a great darkness of, "How can I, and what does it look like, sound like, what does right-speech say, what does right-thought think?"

Attaching yourself to an illumined teacher or master answers all those questions. It is made easy for you. You can observe it, hear it, watch it, see it and fall in love with it through that being. Through falling in love with and attaching yourself to that being as a mother, father, god or a guru, you pass through that being. You learn deeply and merge with that being. You pass through them into your own freedom, a freedom that is actually not owned. It is a true freedom. You pass through that print, that map that that being has offered to you, and you move beyond them and beyond the character of limitation that was you. So, then, we speak of these methods and ways, these suggestions of actions and choices to make, to move your self into the beautiful being of truth.

There is divinity in humanity. But man is unable to realize his innate divinity because of the influence of Maya (illusion). Man should make efforts to recognize his divinity. Only divinity can redeem humanity. Instead of realizing his innate divinity, man is getting entangled in worldliness. What is that we have to experience today? It is divinity, divinity, and divinity alone. It is eternal and is always with you wherever you go. You should never forget this positive power even for a moment. Give up negative feelings and develop faith in the positive power, i.e., divinity.

Sanathan Sarati
May 2004

The kingdom of heaven is like a grain of mustard seed, which a man took and sowed in his field; it is the smallest of all seeds, but when it has grown it is the greatest of shrubs and becomes a tree, so that the birds of the air come and make nests in its branches.

The kingdom of heaven is like leaven, which a woman took and hid in three measures of meal, till it was all leavened.

The kingdom of heaven is like treasure hidden in a field, which a man found and covered up; then in his joy he goes and sells all that he has and buys that field.

Matthew 13.31
Jesus Christ

*I*n summary, these ways and methods of moving yourself from unconsciousness toward consciousness are to study, read, and choose outwardly the Shepherd to follow; to take responsibility and sit in meditative-type action to open the avenues within; to examine what arises in your being in thought and speech; to listen to it non-judgmentally; to watch where it goes; to use the tools of writing if necessary. These ways will suffice and they will engage you in a dharmic existence.

We would then add to this the choosing of sangha, or spiritual community and fellowship, whether it be through a religion or church, or through pure sangha, which is not operating under a religious title but simply sitting in meditative, devotional presence with others. Sangha is studying with others and allowing the friendships and community of those who choose to move themselves into a dharmic place. It is doing this with them, having the support energetically and consciously, and moving through this format of fellowship. Then it is holding non-judgment as a primary choice so that those in your spiritual fellowship can have the masters and the ways that they choose. They can share that and it can be seen as a great oneness, a richness. There is not to be judgment, but just a choosing to sit and be with humanity in this way.

By association with the Holy Ones, attachments drop away, and so are killed the tendencies of mind. When these are gone, a fixity within the Self is found, and Liberation while yet living, gained. Therefore the Holy Ones seek out and serve.

By such association with the Great, the mind is turned within to seek the Self. Through such clear quest the Supreme State is found. That supreme State can never be attained by conning books, through teachers, or by acts however good, or by any other means.

If such association can be had, what is the use o Yogic practices or other discipliners to gain one's end? Would anybody want to use a fan by means of which to make a cooling draught even when a cool breeze from the South Sea blew?

The fiercest heat is cooled by the moon's rays, and destitution can be warded off by the Kalpaka tree; while sins are cleansed by Holy Ganges, these three disappear by the mere vision of a Man o Light. Oh, what is equal unto such a One?

The Poems of Ramana Maharshi

Crossing the Water

We feel this is a moment of poetry. Poetry is bringing through consciousness, with image or song, and speaking directly to the heart. To live in dharma, to choose to become truth, is like crossing the divide, crossing the water. It is saying goodbye to unconsciousness, to limitations, to familiarity, and all that is chosen that keeps one turning in circles, coming into pain and confusion. It is standing there at the edge of that great water, that great plain, and saying, "I'm leaving and I'm going. I'm coming home. I am leaving this world and I'm moving deeper into this world and what it really is. I am leaving illusion and moving into the light."

There is a bell that rings within the soul that says *now - now it is time*. It is a bell that can sometimes be heard ringing distantly, or sometimes as a great gonging – *now, now come to the edge, prepare to say goodbye.* The bell rings and activates the will, mind, emotion and the whole being to move into the beauty of itself and leave behind forever that darkness, that ugliness, the cramped and closed quarters of unconsciousness.

Crossing the waters, one needs to use every footstep, every faculty of one's being. One needs to use one's whole heart, whole mind, and every aspect of what one is - will, body - leaving nothing behind, compromising nothing, nor saying, "I will go with my heart but not my will, or my mind but not my body. I will leave my body behind, and not eat." Crossing the water is not the path of an ascetic who starves the body and never listens to the will. It is for the being who goes with all that they are, in fullness and totality, and brings all that the human being is into divine beingness. That is the crossing.

The crossing is momentous and great. Is it dangerous, vast, or possible? Can it be done? Listen to who asks those questions because it is the self, the emotional, fragmented, smaller self, the egoic nature. The only way to cross the water is to be guided from the hub of the wheel, from the great presence of beingness in the centre of your being and all beings. The only way to navigate and cross is to continually open the channels and listen. There are simple answers, great comforting answers, answers that sound like yes, that resound in laughter. It is who you are all along. It is what you are made of. It is eternally patient and sure.

So who and what are making the crossing? The crossing is a purification of the entire being that would tend to fragment itself into lives, character, mind, emotion, and will, for while fragmented there can be no crossing. There is no such thing as a passage into truth as a fragmented being. A fragmented being is in an unconsciousness of parts - voices speaking, characters, lives, unfinished projects and non-compatible visions and desires. The crossing is a unifying and purifying that organizes the entire being into a living unit so that all the faculties and developments of that being become a unified whole. All the artistry, all the abilities, become woven to the simple presence at the centre - the truth. As this purifying occurs, the crossing is made with greater and greater ease. The crossing of the waters is an experience of joy, moving further and further into expansiveness and light, coming home with eyes and heart open wide - a becoming of truth.

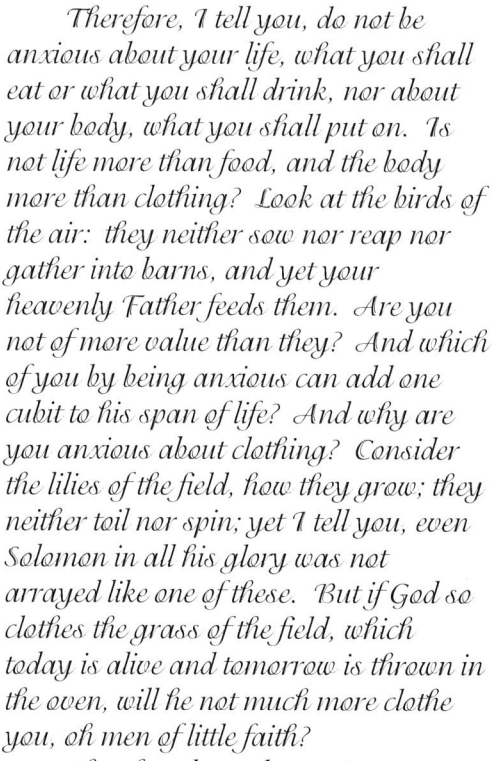

Therefore, I tell you, do not be anxious about your life, what you shall eat or what you shall drink, nor about your body, what you shall put on. Is not life more than food, and the body more than clothing? Look at the birds of the air: they neither sow nor reap nor gather into barns, and yet your heavenly Father feeds them. Are you not of more value than they? And which of you by being anxious can add one cubit to his span of life? And why are you anxious about clothing? Consider the lilies of the field, how they grow; they neither toil nor spin; yet I tell you, even Solomon in all his glory was not arrayed like one of these. But if God so clothes the grass of the field, which today is alive and tomorrow is thrown in the oven, will he not much more clothe you, oh men of little faith?

Therefore do not be anxious, saying, "What shall we eat?" or "What shall we drink?" or "What shall we wear?" For the Gentiles seek all these things; and your heavenly Father knows that you need them all. But seek first his kingdom and his righteousness, and all these things shall be yours as well. Therefore do not be anxious about tomorrow, for tomorrow will be anxious for itself. Let the day's own trouble be sufficient for the day.

Matthew 6.25

Practical Workings With Self

The egoic self has been in development for a long time - many lives including this life. It is a large house sitting heavily on its foundations. We say this to emphasize the largeness, the importance of the self and learning to be in relationship with it, working through and transforming it towards the identity of the divine within form. The self as the house is not to be subject to the wrecking ball, negated or eliminated, for why would there even be 'self'? Why would anything arise within this great creation if it didn't have a place, if it wasn't a truth, a stepping-stone, a rung of the ladder? The stepping-stone needs to be understood and used so that this house becomes a mansion in which every room, every aspect of self, is open to the light and in-filled with purpose. See it this way. Do not struggle with or negate the self, but embrace and hold it as a part of the journey of your formation, a part of who you are.

To work practically with the self, then, is to lovingly understand each aspect of self, infusing and directing it towards the brilliant goal of becoming truth. What is true? What is true before you, in what you think and what you see? From where do we know what is true? Listen to the self. What is true is shaky ground. What is true is heard beyond the self, yet using the self to listen. What is true can be heard in the heart, the core of the being, the soul. Self, then, must learn to listen beyond what arises within it. It must turn its ear towards heart, towards the interior of the being, towards the deep, expansive quietness of meditation, the reaching upwards and yearning of prayer and devotion, listening beyond its house, putting its ears to the window. Truth streams in with the light.

Listen to what arises easily in you with that question - *what is truth?* Before acting on it and saying, "Ah, this is true," weigh that against a deeper listening, against time sat in meditation, hearing the more expansive truth. You will be most surprised to hear the difference in what self thinks is true and what soul finds to be true. Do not stop at only listening to what most easily arises from self. Take it into account and yet go farther, weighing what arose in self with what is found deeper. What is the heart or the centre of your being saying when sitting in immersion, in meditation and in the expansiveness of moving beyond mind, emotion and self?

So we put before you, then, this action of taking note of what self says and yet going another step and listening beyond what self says. Let self see the difference and see how a path, an entire lifetime, can be carved from what is true arising from the self rather that what is actually true, arising from beyond self.

Another meaning, then, of the word dharma is allowing true action, true thought, true understanding to flow into self, into its directives, decisions and actions, keeping the windows open for the light to stream in. This is dharma. Dharma requires a practice, a discipline, if it could be put in such a word, towards keeping the windows open, turning deeper and wider for the answer, the direction and the understanding of what is before you each day, choosing not to create actions, projects, conclusions and inner states based on what self has said, but going farther. Self can create illusions that can be held for lives, that can be built around until one's life is a confused disconnection towards truth.

 What is self then? Self is a way-finder. Self is trying to establish the way, to understand the environment one is in and one's place in it. This trying is valiant. Self is taking its directives and information from mind and emotion, placing that into will. The information the mind receives, the impact in the emotions, and how the mind interprets what the emotions carry all flow into the will. This is a description of self: *the way-finder*. It is finding one's way to be happy, to not be hurt, taking the conclusions of the mind to direct the will, to create safety, protection, happiness, and plenty. See the valiance and importance of self.

 Self, then, which includes mind, emotion, and will, must learn to take the directive from beyond the mind or emotion. This directive must be sought and found in - that which sits beyond the being and flows into each being - what we would call soul, Atma, universal truth, God, grace, or Great Spirit. Find the language that suits you. This is where self must turn to be the way-finder. In practical terms, this means developing a daily practice, a pattern of seeking beyond what arises in mind, emotion, and will to create the life and situation that one is in.

Self is an obedient responder - it responds to the loudest, strongest voice. If the loudest voice is fear, caution, love - whatever speaks the loudest, self will respond and act. What speaks the loudest at present will most likely be mind and human emotion, for that is what is patterned and familiar, what you are surrounded by and what you unconsciously and consciously see everyone doing. One must step apart and begin to develop a louder voice, seeking to hear so that the loudest voice is love itself, truth itself, God itself.

Many do this through prayer and devotion to God in the language and path of their church, faith and religion. They are learning to listen beyond self to what is true and learning to respond, taking the higher directives from God. And yet there are many who are not comfortable in the churches, or with terming the universal presence "God", or with naming it at all. Don't be concerned with having labels and words and paths. Be only concerned with living and becoming truth, learning to attune your being beyond what comes most readily, going into the quietude, the expansion of what is there within you and asking earnestly, "What is best? What is most right? What creates holism, benefiting the most beings with the most grace?" These questions, when applied to decisions, actions, and lives, will direct you beyond what only self would say.

Listen to the centre of your being, which is shared with all-being, "God", "Father", "Universal Grace", or "The

Presence." What is heard there is what graces all beings, brings everything into a unified beauty. It is about the entire creation moving into more beauty and consciousness and away from suffering. One can trust what one hears when it includes all. Whereas if you fine-tune your listening to what arises most easily in self, it is not taking into account the family, community, or world. It is taking into account only itself. Understand that self will direct towards protecting and preserving itself, finding the ways of least resistance, the ways to stay intact, to not starve or be rejected. Understand the primitiveness of the current self. This is not because it is negative; it is only because it arose out of separation, out of need to develop the identity and protect against destruction.

However, when self is given, over and over, as a listening device, as a student and devotee of soul and higher presence, it leaves its crudeness and becomes an instrument of peace, of divine manifestation. Character becomes beauteous, full of fun and joy. Character and self are not to be vanquished or seen to be in the way, but transformed into mediums of divine expression.

You are being asked to transform all aspects of who you think you are as self, emotion, will and character, into who you *truly* are. Practically speaking, it means taking this thread, following it and connecting it to that fabric, watching what arises inside, considering it in light of where it will lead. Where does that thought lead? Does it lead to plenty, abundance, and grace for all? Or does it lead to isolation and separation? Watch what arises and then take the extra step to seek deeper answers and greater understandings. It will come to you as easily as the sunlight pours into a window when you move the curtains because it is yours. Its always has been and always will be. All grace, all truth, the most beneficent and beautiful of understandings and becomings are yours. Therefore, as you develop a practice of listening, opening, and seeking, what is yours comes to you more easily. What comes to you is *you*, who you have been all along. It is what is built into the very foundation of all-becoming, all-creation - **all**. There are none who are exempt, and none who are not deserving or unable to access the greatest of answers, the greatest of becoming.

So, begin a process of listening to what your self says. When you feel yourself in resistance, anger, or upset, don't stop there but pause and ask, "From where has this arisen?" First, you will see the person or situation that has triggered you. Ask further, "Why has this called this feeling forth and what does it mean to me and why am I in this resistance?" Follow that until you hear absolutely, personally, what it is within you, so that the person or situation is no longer even what is being thought of. Instead, the focus is on what is being triggered in you. What are you trying to protect and what is your self actually saying? When you have that understanding, you are beginning to be free and you can rewrite the situation.

You can ask even further, "How can I be free of this inner belief? What is the real and true way to address and believe in this?" Keep seeking until you find the widest, most far-reaching and freeing realization. You have heard why you closed and what you are afraid of. You have heard what erroneous belief you carry within the self. Therefore you can now hear beyond that - the real truth.

An example: If someone reaches to me and asks for attention when I feel I do not have the extra attention to give, that the well within me has no more water in it and I cannot give any more, the self is saying, "I cannot do this. I do not have enough." The self believes that it is empty and is wishing that that person would give instead of ask. Therefore, the response is closed, angry, pushing away. "Don't reach into an empty well! Don't emphasize my emptiness; don't cause the feeling to arise in me that I can't do this! I have no more left. Leave me alone." Now who is to be pointed to? The person who has asked, possibly too much? Or the person who believes they do not have enough to give? You can only address from where you stand. If you believe you do not have enough, then no matter who it is that has asked, it is your task to redirect that belief, to realize the illusion and erroneousness of it. True, self does not have enough to give. Self is a finite well, a finite aspect of beingness. Yet you are not self. You are greater than self and you have access within your being to the eternal, endless well of love, attention, and grace. Therefore, in this example, self must recognize what it believes and move beyond.

Become directed by divine self and give from there. Then the pattern of resistance, anger, and closure is freed. The flow of eternal goodness and grace bathes both giver and the one who has asked for attention. All are lifted. There are none singled out for protection. All are given to. Find your own personal situation.

These are practical ways to work with self: hearing what the self is saying and believing, and transforming, expanding and lifting that beyond its confines. Dharma is right-thought, right-speech, and right-action, but this means nothing without the practical understanding of *how* to have right-thought, right-speech, and right-action. To have dharmic principles within your being means learning practical, continuous methods of examining, listening within, redirecting where one responds from - self to soul; mind and emotion to the greater presence within. Developing patterns and practices on a daily basis so that it is true thought that flows through the self, emotions, and mind.

One can yearn for right-thought and right-action. One can yearn for peace, for freedom, and this is good. But yearning must be accompanied by the practical actions which one does with mind, consciousness and the hours of one's day, subscribing some of those moments towards truth. Imprint, pattern, and reprogram one's being so it listens, attunes and responds to grace, to the presence of God, finding one's own language and images, finding what works. Sometimes a mantra immerses one in true beingness, or sometimes a yoga. Find the path and practice it, without getting complacent within any path but realizing the work involved to transform the psyche, belief patterns, and responses towards dharmic ways.

What does it mean to be awake? The Buddha, when coming into a village, following his awakening and great immersion into becoming truth, was asked, "Are you God?" He said, "No. I am awake." That simple.

Buddha means awakened-one. Consider "awake" - eyes open, entire being open to the sunlight, to the universal, undivided truth that permeates every atom of creation, that is behind every evolution of every being throughout the universe. To be awake is to be in the central stream of what is manifesting throughout all creation - the great unity, God emerging. Awake is unity; asleep is fragmentation. When you are confused or struggling, angry, sad, or tormented, you are not awake. You are struggling in the darkness, trying to find the door in a dark room. Develop your days around being awake, sitting in the inner stillness of your being, letting the mind become quieter, following the breath beyond mind and emotion, listening with all that you are, all the senses, capacities and humanity, beyond the humanity. This is allowing wakefulness to stream in, moving one's whole awareness beyond self. Remember, words can never hold this. You will recognize the moments of being awake. You will treasure them as greater jewels than anything given to you in diamond and gold, and each moment of wakefulness will lead to more, for every cell in your being yearns to be awake - the peace that passes understanding.

The body is made up of five elements and is bound to perish sooner or later but the Indweller has neither birth nor death. The Indweller has no attachment whatsoever and is the eternal witness. In fact, the Indweller who is in the form of Atma is verily God itself.

- Telegu Poem

Human Nature & Divine Nature

What is the difference between the human self-nature and the divine or higher self-nature? What thoughts, impulses and feelings come from each one and how can one discern the difference.

As one grows in awareness of their being, it becomes easier to identify the source, direction, and intention of thoughts and feelings. At the outset there requires much reflection and pondering, asking questions and learning how a self-oriented question feels in your emotion, in your being, and how a divine, higher-natured thought or intention feels in your being.

First, we would say that **you all know**. You all are endowed with the ability to know divine source and truth, and to recognize grace. It is your nature and in recognizing grace, you are recognizing your truth and your self in the greater context of true, eternal nature and source. Begin simply with what feels the most liberating and expansive. What plucks the string within your being of greatness? If you look upon the deeds of great souls, mahatmas, and beings who are in service to humanity, how do you feel? Feel within your being as you look upon their works, hear their messages and see the scale of their goodness. That same feeling is the one you must have when considering your own decisions and actions, or when you try to assess the core intention and source of your thoughts, feelings and decisions. There must be a recognition and a feeling in the heart, a brightness, gratitude and joyousness in the mind and emotions, seeing how all-pervasively right it is from that place within you that knows truth.

This takes practice and attention. This takes an assessment, both before and after, of what one has said, thought, done or intended to do. Where do you feel it? And upon feeling it, what does it satisfy? Does it satisfy you in a small way or a big way? Does it satisfy you for the moment or the day, temporarily, or does it satisfy you for all-time, for your whole life? What is the scale of satisfaction and peace that that deed, decision, or statement gave to you? That which satisfies the human self, the lower nature, is of a temporary origin and smaller sphere - again, usually towards safety, survival, protection and ensuring a place in this earth-realm, society or family. Securing a place is strongly instinctual and comes from the lower, animal-nature. It can be seen both subtly and crudely in its grosser form. Ensuring place can be about emotional survival, emotional safety, or psychological security. These are of a higher nature in the human being and yet still arise from the instinct to survive from the lower self-nature.

Divine nature is not concerned with survival, safety or protection. It is not concerned with having a place, for its inherent place is the Great Presence and Beingness of which it is a part. There is no fear of death, ostracism, rejection, or abandonment. Divine nature is ultimately free of human nature and instinctual, animal nature. It is in a brilliant freedom without these concerns that arise from physical embodiment and evolution.

A simple formula can be placed before you. In a sense, it means creating a place for all beings and softly moving into that creation. **Have the intention towards all beings first**, which then secures your place eternally, **rather than seeking your place first as an individual** at the expense or without thought of all beings. There is, then, a very essential core difference between that which arises from instinctual, animal, human nature, i.e. "me first", and the light-filled, spiritual, higher nature, "all beings first". If you were to attend to your own being and what arises within it with this simple formula, you would understand.

Of course, expect that much will arise from your instinctual, human nature that wants good work, enough pay, food, and safety. This is the context you are in. Yet we say to you, you can live within this context with ultimate safety and abundance. Operating your being from its higher divine nature opens the doors of abundance and places you in an energetic sphere that is infused with the reality of beauty and truth where fear does not touch. We only begin to place words to this reality of divine nature that is ultimately free of suffering and fear. Your goal is to move into that identity, to take it as yours, even if only for the original reasons of security, safety, and having a place that is forever true and beautiful. Even if those are the reasons, which they will be, once that reality of the divine character enters into your being, those intentions and thoughts fade away. The main force behind true intention is to gather more and more beings into the light, to create opportunity for those who are suffering to be free of suffering.

If you were to realize the tremendous grace, abundance, and joy that is truly your essential nature! It is your unconscious source and is the great goal of evolution and of your being, to make that which was unconscious and naïve become conscious, wise and full of knowing. Could we then say that selflessness nurtures the human self?

The journey towards divine nature nurtures the human self like a flood of sunlight, like nutrition that is unparalleled. It is not to be divided by saying, "How must I care for my little, human self over here and still be in service and have a spiritual progression and nurturing for this entire humanity over here?" It is not separate. It is not to be placed in separate rooms. To create separation is to create struggle. It is all one. You will nurture your human character by devoting it to its divine nature. You will nurture your human self by placing your efforts and life towards becoming the divine self, seeing all beings as equal, as part of you. What you do for another, you do for all, and what you do for all, you do for you. Nurture others and you are nurtured in return. What you pour outward in love and grace is received by the human self. Why? Because you are *all that*. Again, what is the underlying truth of the golden rule: *do unto others as you would have them do unto you*? Why? Because you are all that.

The Scope Of Becoming Truth As An Awakened Being

This question opens up into the guidance a silence. It is essentially an unanswerable question because of the scale of that which it addresses, the billions and billions of points of God, the individual beings that have within their will-nature a thread of their own evolution. It is unanswerable because of the great web, the interplay of all beings, assisting each other forward and creating limitations for each other.

And yet, to any individual that asks oneself this question, it is answerable. Why? Because within the thread and sphere of your individual nature, it is possible for you to take this into your own grasp, to pour your entire intention and lifetime towards the unfoldment of true beingness. Then, even if the great humanity about you stumbles in unconsciousness, you, Point of God, individual thread, have risen brilliant. Yet you are still bound by the great web, and your full experience of absolute consciousness becoming truth will be held in the great oneness. This is the unfoldment of all creation. The answer is utterly simple. Within your being it is answerable. Within the great oneness it is unanswerable.

And yet we laugh, a million years of laughter at simplicity that is profoundly difficult. How can something simple be so difficult? The door is right before you. It is not locked. The door is your breath, your heart, your essential nature. It is in your origins. It is held in the dying moments that you witness and the birth moments that you host. The door is right before you and if you turn your whole being's attention and purpose toward finding it, it opens quietly. Once opened, that which you have been seeking is all there - the illumined being, the illumined nature, the truth.

  Yet to pass through the door, even when found and opened quietly, requires the ultimate shedding of all illusion, limitation and fear, all that is held within the illusory will-nature, the egoic, instinctual self. One cannot pass through the door clothed; one can only pass through the door naked, bared to the core, to the light. Therefore, it is utterly difficult and the willingness and readiness within your being must be there. There is no pretending. You cannot be an ascetic and starve yourself life after life in order to be that naked. Nakedness is a consciousness, a true wisdom of readiness, not a will-determined readiness, or an outward showing to all mankind that one is ready. The door opens quietly when it is time.

Enter by the narrow gate; for the gate is wide and the way is easy, that leads to destruction, and those who enter by it are many. For the gate is narrow and the way is hard, that leads to life, and those who find it are few.

Matthew 7.13

Therefore, put down this question in peace, and be in peace with every breath and every step and every being. Do not try to place time span or measurement on the great unfolding of the perfect flower, for it will only occur in the exactitude of rightness, of readiness, in the quiet moment when all is in place. It cannot be forced, or pushed, or placed in the greenhouse and given extra nutrients. It must unfold unnoticed in the morning sunlight, in the natural conditions of its own evolution, for it to be strong and bear the seeds for more perfect formations of beingness. If there is push, yearning, impatience, then it is not a true flowering. There must be a wise allowing that knows that when such a perfect flower unfolds, it unfolds forever. It unfolds in immeasurable strength and it changes that being utterly and forever.

I also remember in ancient times, for 500 lifetimes, I practiced transcendent endurance by not being caught up in the idea of a self, a person, a living being, or a life span. So, Subhuti, when a bodhisattva gives rise to the unequalled mind of awakening, he has to give up all ideas. He cannot rely on forms when he gives rise to that mind, nor on sounds, smells, tastes, tactile objects, or objects of mind. He can only give rise to that mind that is not caught up in anything. "How does it feel consciously to exist in the identity as awakened nature or Supreme Being?"

The Diamond That Cuts Through Illusions

How does it feel to consciously exist as awakened nature or supreme being? We smile again at the unanswerable quality of this question, which we could answer by inserting into your consciousness the awareness of this experience. And yet it is wordless and unrecordable. Only its shapes could be given to the mind and human words. And so, in the context of this book of words, we give shape and shadow. Omniscience is the experience of being *all* beings. There is not a personal heart and personal place of feeling. There is not a sense of self encapsulated away from all other selves. There is only a stream of presence that runs through mind and heart, an organizing towards action, knowing, feeling, and communication. Upon requirement and need, there is the pulling inwards towards this stream to create a being that appears separate, that engages in action and giving.

The Buddha Field

"Attempting to describe this is like attempting to describe a single movement in dance" ~ Thoenn Glover

Once the requirement from this field of human beingness, this sphere of animal and nature beings, has passed, there is expansiveness, absolute peace, the essence of joy that sits like a brilliant, quiet sunlight. There is the sense of a vast field of presence which all beings travel through, where all is known and yet the knowing is a peace-filled entire presence of consciousness. Within an intentional breath of manifesting Supreme Being, divine embodiment, within the human form, there is movement towards engagement with the material realm. Mind, speech, heart, will, and form are utilized towards actions and creations for the purpose of embodying the divine character. The divine embodiment manifests to further, heal, and teach mankind. There is no ownership or individual pride towards anything that is created through the stream of manifesting divine nature through human nature. It is like an inversion, placing the great, expansive field of presence within containers and forms where it can be accessed by those more bound to smaller conscious states.

The in-breath draws in the vast expansion of Supreme Being; the out-breath blows that into the shapes and forms of manifestation. There are no dreams, unconsciousness, pockets, or corners of that which is not part of the great field of light. There are no shadows or eddies. There is utter and absolute peace, light and presence. The entire purpose of manifesting in form - creating character, giving voice, and executing decisions - is only to create umbrella, place, and shape to the qualities and meaning of divine reality. There is no death, transitions, or change, but rather absolute freedom of the physical form. It is an eternal summer. The body may be pained or not pained, may be worn and shed without notice or trauma. There is no attachment. The presence is in absolute protection and needs no shaping, process, or movement. Peace is an absolute stillness.

In the absolute nature of beingness, there is no self. Self is shaped only as a vessel of beauty. It contains words that guide those who are lost, a vessel of the sweetness and warm fragrance of love to be given to those who are forsaken and those who yearn to know love. It is character, voice, conjecture, creation, and manifestation. Self is a vessel to pour the sweet water of truth into the cups of those who reach for it. It is a mirage, temporary and fleeting, a shape that the stream may pass through so that it may be observed, tasted and known. Without the vessel, the stream would not be experienced by the human being. The vessel is a passing shape to house divine nature within, to give it voice and presence, coalesced into a nature that can be seen by those trapped and still evolving in human nature and form.

As the temporary self dissolves, the divine nature has no need of self. Its shape is endless, its vessel all creation and beyond. And yet it needs the shape of all creation and bears the vessel of human nature. It needs this to manifest divine nature in increasing knowledge and consciousness so that all creation, as it passes through lives and deaths, shaping molecules into form, opens its eyes wide in awakening and says - *I am*. The most beautiful and brilliant '*I am*.' Then there is no more need for the vessel. It moves into a brilliance of form beyond physical, molecular creation, and this is beyond the question.

"Subhuti, if someone were to offer an immeasurable quantity of the seven treasures to fill the worlds as infinite as space as an act of generosity, the happiness resulting from that virtuous act would not equal the happiness resulting from a son or daughter of a good family who gives rise to the awakened mind and reads, recites, accepts, and puts into practice this sutra, and explains it to others, even if only a gatha of four lines. In what spirit is this explanation given? Without being caught up in signs, just according to things as they are, without agitation. Why is this?

"All composed things are like a dream, a phantom, a drop of dew, a flash of lightning. That is how to meditate on them, that is how to observe them."

After they heard the Lord Buddha deliver this sutra, the Venerable Subhuti, the bhiksus, the bhiksunis, laymen and laywomen, and gods and asuras, filled with joy and confidence, undertook to put these teachings into practice.

Dhammapada

Self Acceptance

Central to the journey of becoming truth is full acceptance of and being present to each step, each day, each stage one's own being is in, each situation, effort and result. In acceptance lies absorption, integration, and a maturing depth that allows all that has been gathered to build into the being a stronger foundation for new growth and effort. It is not to be seen as a far-off goal, a door that one constantly paces in front of trying to learn how to open, or an illuminated mountaintop with endless miles of journeying towards. It is defeating to place that separation and unattainable nature upon yourself. Your effort is not for tomorrow or the next life. Your effort is to bear fruit, to be at peace with what is, *now*. This means peace with who you are, how you have developed thus far, what you have done, and exactly what you were capable of doing, understanding, and taking in that was new. Self-acceptance is practicing perfect peace, which allows each moment and effort to be complete, not needing it to be more or less. Realize the journey is long and wonderful and the stages are many; they grow upon each other through days and years and lives.

Do not lose heart and energy into thinking of tomorrow as better than today, as where you will find happiness and peace, and continually addressing this effort so that its fruit is felt later, not now. This is unsustainable, and not the wisdom of this teaching. Place your effort of realizing truth and then sit with it in peace, treasuring every fruit and step, no matter how small. This means being able to say, "This was enough for now."

This does not mean an end to continuing effort and practice. Being at peace and acceptance with your being as it is does not mean stagnation or stillness. It is not an ending or a stopping place. Rather, it is the most perfect place to take the next step forward. And why? Because then the next step is more easily directed into a pure realizing of higher intention. It is a firmer, fuller step that is not pushed by regret, self-dislike, or self-criticism. It is a true step in inner development in that there is more space and ability to fully realize what came before and what must come next. There is more patience and love with the process, and love for the self and all others on the journey.

To take the next step from a place of self-dislike, self-reproach, non-peace and non-acceptance is a grasping, a grabbing, a pushing and willing forward to improve one's relationship to one's self, pitting and measuring one's self against an image, ideal, or teaching. Sometimes the measurement works out well, but often it doesn't. This is not sustainable, and though the movement forward is true and intact, it is not as solidly implanted and understood.

Understand the importance of self-acceptance and practice it. Practice being here, at peace with this, reflecting on what one has done in one's life and having compassion for all that has led one to this place, this state of being. Realize the factors that have led you to where you are and be at peace with them. Accept them. Do not regret what has led you to be what you are now. Rather, have a compassionate acceptance. This will then free you of that which appears to have been a mistake or negative or caused pain in others or in yourself. To have compassionate acceptance will free you more surely from the conditions of the past than to have self-regret and non-acceptance. Understand that to move forward more wholly and freely is to be in compassionate self-acceptance to all that has come before.

Reflect on what has come before. Use the wisdom of hindsight and see how this led to that and that led to this. Do so not with self-criticism or regret, but with compassionate non-attachment, realizing what your being was capable of and what it created. From that basis of self-understanding and acceptance, one can begin to step forward more surely, correctly and truly.

We cannot overemphasize this teaching, this need to be at peace with your being at whatever stage it is on the journey, being able to find the bench and sit and breathe into a deep peace of where you've come. You may see the rocky, steep path that led to the bench, and you may see a rocky path leading away from it. Yet sitting there and resting deeply into where you find yourself, what you have become and created - this eases your journey, paving the way forward so that you flow more easily and fully into this great passage of becoming truth.

Becoming Truth: A Dynamic, Active Process

There is no mountaintop where you stop and have 'become'. It is a *becoming*, a movement, like music, always forward, developing into a finer sound, dynamic and alive. As you enjoin with greater and greater beauty, becoming light-filled presence, expansive, spacious and beautiful beyond words, you enter the peace beyond understanding. You see that existence is not static. It is an unfolding, a deepening, refined, exquisite journey.

Accept your being on this journey. Accept the point where it lightly stands, being open to what was before and what is ahead, and in love with the being you are and the being you are a part of - the great presence of beauty, truth, and grace. Supreme beingness is an ever-growing and becoming presence. It flows through your eyes, the veins of plants, the underground rivers of the earth, the explosions of stars. It holds all beauty and pain, all darkness and light. It holds all that you are, primally and in the full expansion of consciousness.

Understand and let yourself be a part of this - a child, a builder, a part of the great orchestra, no matter how small or how great a part you feel you have been given. Simply *be* a part of the great anthem of joyous becoming. In peace, we leave this with you.

As I am pure Existence, I am not the
body or the senses, mind or life, or even
ignorance, for all these things are quite
insentient and so unreal.

As there is not a second consciousness
to know Existence, it must follow that
Existence is itself that consciousness; So I
myself am that same consciousness.

In their real nature as Existence both
Creatures and the Creator are the same.
The Unique Principle. In attributes and
knowledge only is a difference found.

If one can only realize at Heart what
one's true nature is, one then will find that
'tis Infinite Wisdom, Truth and Bliss,
without beginning and without an end.

    The Poems of Ramana Maharshi

In the morning of this day of days
I quietly sit and feel
the freshness of the air,
the soft song of birds freely sung
upon the young morning light.
All is before me,
a lovely unknown of possibilities,
a thousand unopened flowers.

In the noon of this day of days,
I am walking without ceasing,
through an air filled with smells
and shapes of thoughts.
Everything is speaking,
saying what must be said,
except the birds who are silent.
All is around me
and under and above.
I carry the weight,
the bright angles of light,
the full colours of a thousand flowers
opening.

In the evening of this day of days,
I find the edge of sea,
the waves upon waves
pulling footprints and debris
back into the depths.
The light is gathering silver and golden
into itself, the Sun.
All is behind me
and some evening
the waves may gather me
along with the thousand flower petals
strewn on the sand.

Jean

ISBN 1412071178